MACCLESFIELD EXPOSED!

Vic Barlow

Published by Sigma Leisure – an imprint of
Sigma Press, 1 South Oak Lane, Wilmslow,
Cheshire SK9 6AR, England.

British Library Cataloguing in Publication Data
A CIP record for this book is available from the British Library.

ISBN: 1-85058-765-5

Typesetting and Design by: Sigma Press, Wilmslow, Cheshire.

Cover Design: Graham Beech

Cover Cartoon and illustrations: Brian Sage

The photographs on pages 15 and 17 are the copyright of the Advertiser Group of Newspapers.

Printed by: MFP Design & Print

Introduction

When numerous people suggested that I write a book I was flattered, but didn't take it seriously. Fate has a habit of kicking me in the teeth if I get too self absorbed. It was with this in mind that I considered such a project something of a step too far in the self-appreciation stakes. However none of us is inured to the influences of others and when I received a few letters encouraging me to 'have a go' the book came back to the top of my agenda.

By way of confirmation a new postman called at our home and asked me to sign for a recorded delivery. He looked down at my signature and winked " Vic Barlow?" I nodded, "Macc Express?" I nodded again.

"Funny mate, bloody funny, makes us all laugh at the Sorting Office!" and he disappeared down the drive whistling "If I were a rich man".

"That's it, it's a sign," I thought and was now more determined than ever to make my book a reality. I should have known better!

My son called me on the phone to catch up with events and I was explaining about the book. "You will let me have a copy won't you dad?" he enquired.

"Yes, of course." I was positively beaming down the phone.

"Make it around 70 to 80 pages will you?"

"Why so precise?" I asked, curiously.

"The coffee table keeps wobbling and a book that size under one leg would be perfect."

The bubble burst yet again. However, fate works both ways. During the spring of 2000, Mike Quilley, the editor of the Macc Express, invited me to do a weekly column and writing fever really kicked in.

I had no difficulty in finding topics around Macc; in fact, my only problem was that I was restricted to one page! I discussed the book concept yet again with Pat Hills, my mentor down at the Macc Express office and both she and Mike gave me their wholehearted support. Graham Beech, at Sigma Press painstakingly corrected my schoolboy mistakes and designed the cover to enable 'Macclesfield Exposed!' to finally see the light of day.

Mrs B was, as always, a great source of inspiration. I did a lot of my writing during the night and, each morning, she would retire to the bathroom to read and review every page I had written. I never got any of it back from her though – I have no idea what she did with it, other than she kept requesting that I use less shiny paper!

The first part of the book is all new material and I have included a number of wonderful stories involving local characters that, apart from a small amount of artistic licence, are basically true. The second part is a collection of my letters and articles published in the Macc Express in, as near as I can recall, date order. They are accompanied by some lively illustrations drawn by local cartoonist and well-known computer phobic Brian Sage.

I hope you enjoy reading it as much as I enjoyed writing it and Macclesfield Council enjoyed burning it!

If you also enjoy the book, please tell your friends.

If you don't — please tell 'em that you did!

Vic Barlow

Contents

Part 1: For The Love of Macc!

I came to Macclesfield as a young innocent but was soon exposed to some of the most colourful characters on God's earth. Over the years they've nailed me inside a used coffin, locked me in the village stocks and chopped my lounge to bits.

Come on, I'll tell you all about it …

By the Scruff of my Neck

It was in May 1965 that my love affair with Macclesfield began. I'd applied for the position of Trainee Sales Representative at Neckwear in Grosvenor Street and I got the job. I was 19 years old and so excited that I forgot to mention at the interview that I couldn't drive—a fairly basic requirement for a Travelling Salesman.

As the days ticked away towards the commencement of my employment, I rehearsed over and over again how I was going to break the news of my lack of legitimate driving skills to my new employer. I had already started driving lessons, in a manner of speaking, not with The British School of Motoring but with Dave's Driving School. Dave offered his services for 10 shillings an hour, which was less than half that of other driving schools, due to the fact that most sessions involved chauffeuring him home paralytic from Denton Liberal Club which doubled as his dubious 'office'.

On my first day I arrived by train all the way from Denton and reported in to the Sales Manager, a genial gentleman called Ron Hardy who wore his hair Brylcreemed straight back with a central parting, sported a moustache of the Terry Thomas variety and referred to everyone as 'Old Boy'.

It was obvious that there was no real training plan in place and, for lack of any better idea, I was assigned to Fabric Inspection, an incredibly boring task involving examining yard after yard of fabric as it passed from one roller to another, looking for and marking knitting 'faults'. This was not what I had anticipated. However, I was determined to make a good show of it on my first day but fate was to take another turn and, just before lunchtime, a visiting senior buyer from a very important department store came along on a grand tour of inspection. Flanked by all the Neckwear Top Brass she approached me and demanded to know *exactly* what I thought I was doing.

"I'm … er … inspecting fabric Miss," I replied as if to a school mistress.

"Well, you are not doing a very good job," she barked loud enough for the whole of Macclesfield to hear. The Top Brass shuddered.

"Look at these faults here," she bellowed, "Are you blind?" Without waiting for my response, she flung her handbag to the floor and pushed me out of the way, grabbed the needle and brightly coloured wool used for marking the faults out of my hand and began to weave it into almost every square foot of fabric as she screamed

"Fault here ... and here ... another one there ... and here ... and there ..."
In less than five minutes she had marked more knitting 'faults' than I had found in a whole morning. She then went on to interrogate and humiliate in turn almost every man in the knitting shed before retrieving her handbag and retreating to the management toilet for a midday replenishment of war paint.

A peculiar atmosphere followed her withdrawal. The Brass huddled together in one corner presumably licking their wounds and an eerie stillness pervaded the weaving shed until ... a primeval scream pierced the building. The Brass went into full alert and bolted for the door just as the receptionist flew through it shouting for all to hear that our Queen Buyer had flounced into the executive toilet and opened her handbag only to find a dead mouse where her make up should have been.

The Buyer was given brandy and oodles of sympathy and taken out by the now totally subservient Brass for a large, expensive lunch while the knitting shed settled back into its usual steady hum of activity marked only by the smug look of gratification on the faces of the guilty knitters.

I was glad to get back to the uneventful monotony of fabric inspection but it wasn't long before Mr Hardy sent for me and to my utter amazement flung the keys to his brand new Vauxhall Victor in my direction giving me a list of small deliveries he wanted me to make around town. This was not a good time to tell my new boss I couldn't drive and anyway, hadn't Drunken Dave's Driving School taught me something?

I took the keys with trepidation and found the gleaming new car on the Staff car park. Carefully I placed my deliveries in the boot, unlocked the driver's door and to my horror saw that it was column change with the gear lever just beneath the steering wheel. I had never even been inside a vehicle with column change, let alone driven one.

Men from the knitting shed, standing outside on a smoke break, waved at me and jeered. There was no escape, I slid along the bench seat and sat behind the wheel.

"Gentlemen start your engines," shouted one of the knitters in the manner in which Grand Prix races of the day commenced, then guffawed along with his mates.

"Come on Stirling," yelled another "start her up, let's see what she can do."

Bang ... Crunch...Bang ... I found first gear and kangarooed out of the car park. This car was Mr Hardy's pride and joy, and common sense told me not to push my luck, especially considering the unfortunate events of earlier in the day.

My first delivery was round the corner at the top of Chestergate and I parked the car (still not yet out of first gear) partly on the pavement outside the UCP Restaurant, a famous purveyor of tripe.

When I returned I could not summon up the courage to drive it away again in full view of the watching public and so I decided to leave it exactly where it was and deliver all my packages on foot.

As they were all small parcels of fabric for home-workers they were bulky but not heavy and I completed all my deliveries without incident. When I finally returned to the car a large Constable was leaning against it just about to write down the registration.

"Afternoon young sir," he greeted me.

"Oh, hello officer."

"This your car?"

"No, it belongs to my boss," I replied.

"Well, will your boss be pleased to know that you've had it illegally parked causing an obstruction for over three hours?"

"No he won't. I'll probably get the sack." I said truthfully, trying not to think of my driving licence predicament.

"Well, if your Fairy Godmother could grant you a wish what would it be?" he asked incredulously.

"To not get booked and go back to work."

"And if I were your Fairy Godmother would you do something for me?"

I didn't like the way this conversation was going but I had no choice "Yes, of course officer," I replied nervously.

"Well sir would you mind removing your hat?"

It was a rule at Neckwear that all Sales Personnel should wear a hat, regardless of how ridiculous it might look. I took off the trilby. He held it in his large palms and inspected it thoroughly.

"Is this hat yours?"

"No. Actually, it belongs to my father," I replied.

"Ah that explains it. I couldn't think why a young lad of your age would wear an old-fashioned trilby three sizes too big.

"We've had a theft reported from the UCP here," he indicated by pointing his thumb over his shoulder, "but it turned out to be a load of tripe," and he threw back his head and brayed with laughter.

"What do you do for a living then?" he inquired.

"Sales representative," I offered tentatively.

"Well here you go then and be on your way," he offered me back the hat. "And try not to wear it out talking through it." I left him standing on the pavement still laughing heartily at his own joke.

It was hard to believe, as I sat on the train going home, that so many bizarre things could happen in one day. Despite my public humiliations, I laughed out loud enough for other passengers in the carriage to hear and edge uncomfortably away. In that first day I had learned nothing about salesmanship as I had hoped. But I had witnessed what can be achieved by the selective placement of a dead rodent and that, in Macclesfield, the Laughing Policeman was alive and well.

I guffawed to myself but louder this time and my fellow passengers glanced at each other with frightened expressions as if they had a lunatic in their midst.

"Macclesfield, Macclesfield, I've been to Macclesfield" I explained to no one in particular and the other passengers all nodded knowingly as though I'd just been 'let out' and went back to their evening newspapers.

Letters Begin ...

I can't remember when I first started writing letters to the Macclesfield Express but I'll never forget some of the *brilliant* stories that inspired me. Like the political debate surrounding the damage to young trees in Macclesfield caused by deer straying from Lyme Park and stripping their bark.

At a Council meeting, the full extent of the damage was discussed and a solution sought. Should a higher fence be erected around the Park? Should a new fence be erected around the trees? The Council was caught in a dilemma. What should be done? Fence the Park? Fence the trees?

And then, as if by Divine Inspiration, came a suggestion from a councillor so stunningly obvious that it bedevilled belief that no one had thought of it before ... lion dung! He reasoned that as deer are terrified of lions, their droppings placed at the base of every tree would naturally scare the deer away. A huge swell of approval ensued, but the question of whether generations of deer brought up within shouting distance of the Grosvenor Centre carried the same innate terror of wild cats as their brothers and sisters roaming the Serengeti was overlooked in the euphoria of so simple a solution.

Lion dung won the day.

The mathematics of this whole exercise intrigued me. I was clearly no arithmetic genius but, even allowing for some miscalculation, I could work out that in Macclesfield Forest there were probably around a million trees. And, within a forty-mile radius of Macclesfield (the optimum distance I was assured for the transportation of fresh lion dung) there were only two lions, both of whom resided at Chester Zoo.

Even if these poor unfortunate creatures were fed laxatives for the rest of their natural lives, I doubted whether they would have been up to the job. My imagination began to run amok. Maybe Macclesfield Garden Centre would soon be cashing in on this unfulfilled demand among local gardeners.

"I'll have two sacks of bark chippings and a large bag of lion dung please."

"Would that be African Lion sir or Mountain?"

"Oh ... er ...African please."

"Mature male or young female?"

"Male, please. It's for my Leylandii."

I don't know what the final outcome was but Macclesfield Garden Centre never did get their act together and take advantage of the huge demand created by that simple yet effective idea from one of Maccles-field's finest councillors. More surprisingly, it was never given a mention on Gardeners' World.

Happy Hour

I thought this story could never be topped until from Prestbury, one of our leafier glades, came this barnstormer of an idea 'Drinking Lessons for Teenagers'. This concept apparently came from the notion that teenagers needed help and education in learning how to drink alcohol and were cor-dially invited to a meeting in Prestbury where some well-meaning soul was going to show them how to do it.

I have no idea what ensued other than to say it must have been a huge success as I now see gangs of teenagers roaming all over the Borough swigging cider and strong lager from bottles and cans as if their very life depends on it.

Thanks for that, Prestbury.

Feeling Hot! Hot! Hot!

Macclesfield's wonderful sense of irony has always been a source of joy and very few weeks go by without something occurring which in any other town would appear ludicrous. But I must say that even I was taken by sur-prise that day in 1997, when I read in the Macclesfield Express that we had an official Tourist Office in our town with a staff of four.

Macclesfield might well be a wondrous, magical place to you and I – but what would be its attractions to the outside world I wondered? I could see thousands of holidaymakers planning their next vacation on Teletext. At least we would be easy to find in the alphabetical listings ... right alongside Marbella and Majorca, but was that enough?

I need not have worried. An absolute blockbuster of an idea was already taking place within the council chamber. An idea so stunning in its conception that I could see Euro Disney throwing in the towel and retreat-ing across the Atlantic.

What was this breathtaking innovation that would see tourists from

... WELL, THAT'S ENOUGH OF THE CONVEYOR BELT...
WHY DON'T WE GO AND HAVE A LOOK AT THE FURNACE?

around the globe flocking to our town? Open Day at Macclesfield Crematorium. I'll say it again just in case you don't believe me. Open Day at
Macclesfield Crematorium!

Even I was stunned. What sort of experience was an Open Day at a crematorium going to be? I could see coach loads of pensioners with cameras
and open-toed sandals standing around in groups, while a council
employee gave them a guided tour.

"On the left you'll see the furnace where you'll all be incinerated. It has
been completely renovated and it's said that temperatures can rise to over
300 degrees Centigrade, providing we have a good supply of nutty slack.

"And over here is the chute we'll be sliding you down."

Even by Macclesfield standards, this had to be a World-Beater.

Walking Back to Happiness

Then we had that masterpiece of planning when the Council decided it was
time the town centre was pedestrianised and, after two hundred and fifty
years of waiting, dug up Market Square almost overnight. I happened to be
there in the rain, when some poor unfortunate bride who obviously had not
been warned about such an event ran splish-splashing through the puddles. Her bridesmaids trudged dutifully behind in the mud to St. Michael's
Church while the wedding cars were forced to wait 100 yards away down
Jordangate.

I was too embarrassed to hang around in case I saw a funeral coming

up the 108 Steps! I mean, they could hardly carry a coffin up Mill Street straight past McDonalds could they?

Your Lucky Number is ...

Then we had that wonderful story about a Ladies Barber Shop Quartet who were looking for additional members as their 'numbers had declined to below forty'. Personally, I always thought forty was just about the optimum number for a quartet.

Another man with mathematical problems was Tony Wilkinson, the Manager of Rainow Cubs Seven-a-Side soccer team who went right through all the preliminary rounds of a 1997 knockout competition and made it into the final before someone noticed that they were actually playing with *eight* men.

You would have thought that Tony might have noticed something odd when he was giving out the numbered shirts but, as Tony later admitted, "Arithmetic has never been my thirty-nine."

Express yourself

The Macclesfield Express has contributed greatly to Macclesfield's reputation for madness and eccentricity. When, in 1996, Macclesfield Town F.C. was promoted to the Third Division, the good old Express had a beautiful photograph of the Team celebrating in the dressing room plastered right across the front page. Unfortunately the editorial Team failed to notice what everyone in Macclesfield couldn't miss, namely that one member of this championship winning team was in a state of undress and revealing his tackle for all to see. Boy, was that edition soon sold out!

One of my recent favourites is the photo of a well-known Macclesfield councillor waving at the camera as he sets off on a charity walk and beneath it the headline from some totally unrelated story 'Flasher exposes himself then waves Good Bye'.

The Waters Green Sting

Another amazing coincidence occurred in the late seventies when some author of dubious intent decided to write a Guide to British Public Toilets and wrote of Macclesfield:

"The town's deluxe lavatories can be found on Churchill Way where there is hot and cold running water and a regular attendant on duty plus facilities for the disabled." Doesn't that sound wonderful?

Unfortunately, what it failed to point out was, that at the time of its publication, Macclesfield Police Force was carrying out an exercise to find out *exactly* what was going on in our public toilets. They had strategically stationed themselves on the roof of every loo in town, peering down through skylights to check if the toilets were being used for the purpose intended.

After numerous cock-ups they received a tip-off from a local super-grass and police attention was concentrated on Waters Green toilets where arrests for 'indecent behaviour' were soon made. When the cases came up in court and the daring exploits of Macclesfield Police fully exposed it emerged that the policeman in charge of the 'Waters Green Sting' as it later became known was an officer with the ingenious name of DC John Thomas.

That is why to this day you can always tell a Macclesfield man on holiday. He's the one in the gents with the wet shoes staring nervously up at the ceiling.

Dogged Determination

Another brilliant Macclesfield policeman was PC John Williams, a Rainow resident and dog handler of considerable experience. When in 1980 his veteran canine partner was retired PC Williams was allocated a young but already huge German Shepherd dog and was sent off to the Police Dog Training Centre for the appropriate bonding period. Almost immediately on his return to duty he was called to a Prestbury house in the dead of night where a break-in had been reported. Arriving at the scene in his police van,

PC Williams spotted intruders climbing over a perimeter wall and immediately leapt out of his vehicle and released his dog with the fearsome command of "Get them". Unfortunately, the dog, who had only just been taught the Queen's English, was still a little shaky on pronouns and misinterpreted the order as "Get me!".

Now, in fairness to the dog, from that point on it was fearless in the execution of its duty and dragged PC Williams around the grounds for ages until they both fell into the outdoor swimming pool. PC William's reputation as a top dog trainer had been made very early in his career when a senior officer lost a gold pen in South Park and had summoned the constable to his office to ask if his dog could find it. The nervous young dog handler tried to explain that South Park held a lot more interesting scents with which to tantalise his dog but, as the pen in question was a present from the Senior Officer's wife, his observations were brushed aside and he was ordered to 'Get out there and look'.

Fortunately for PC Williams, within minutes of commencing his futile search the precious pen was handed to him by a passer-by who had just picked it up off the footpath. He and his dog returned triumphant but wisely kept tight-lipped about their method of search.

From that point on, he was known among senior officers as a dog trainer of unbelievable skill. A reputation which served him well throughout his entire career, despite the fact that on subsequent occasions both dog and handler failed to locate a missing shire-horse, a stolen pig and numerous unwashed fugitives. Presumably, in the course of resolving his pronoun problem, the dog had lost his sense of smell.

A Coffin Fit

In the early seventies, I became a member of Rainow Players — a small village drama group set up more to satisfy the unfulfilled theatrical ambitions of its founder members than to entertain the general public.

We did quite well for a time, performing light comedy and even wrote a three-act play ourselves, which was really two and a half hours of jokes strung together with a bit of dialogue. Although Saturday nights were usually full houses we always struggled to sell tickets for Thursday and Friday.

A pragmatic section of the membership, of which I liked to be considered one, wanted to "give 'em what they want" — which basically meant comedy. This was not the reason our founders had started a 'Theatre Group' (as they liked to call it) and in a moment of commercial madness we agreed to do a set of plays of such dire content that even Sir Laurence Olivier would have failed to make entertaining.

Although our producer had the time of her life, for the cast it was a painful and embarrassing experience played to bored and restless audiences.

In one play, the Prompt, responsible for following the dialogue from the wings and making sure that any cast member who had forgotten their place was given the right cue, dozed off and subsequently gave an incorrect prompt, skipping several pages of dialogue.

The result of this was that in the final act when two detectives dramatically arrived on stage to arrest the murderer everyone knew *who* had done it, but no one knew *what* he had done. The several pages skipped by our slumbering Prompt had contained that part of the story in which The Murder had been committed.

This was baffling enough to an already bewildered audience but the victim of the murder, whose body should have been carried from the stage early in Act Three, was still sitting on the sofa, large as life, smoking a pipe.

Our audiences were at an all-time low and shrinking. Even families and friends of cast members could no longer be relied upon to fill seats. We were attempting to sell tickets door-to-door around the village, competing with the Jehovah's Witnesses in the popularity stakes (and losing) — when a local farmer regaled us with his ideas on what should be done.

"Entertain 'em," he bellowed. "Give 'em summet to laugh at instead of all that drama crap," he added unceremoniously and then went back to his milking. A kernel of an idea had been planted.

In 1973 we put on our first Rainow cabaret evening, which meant recruiting anyone who could sing, dance, juggle or play an instrument and endeavoured to put them altogether in some sort of rag-tag variety show. As the only one with any claim to experience in this area, I agreed to be producer and compère.

The theme of our cabaret was 'The Roaring Twenties' with the men all dressed as Mafia gangsters, while the girls became Flappers and performed the Charleston. After boring our audience to death during our 'Shakespearean' period I thought it may be difficult to sell tickets but helpers and friends that had witnessed the rehearsals had put the word around that this could be fun and ticket sales were excellent. For the first time ever, we also had a Licensed Bar.

It was vital that the show got off to a flying start and we brainstormed for several drunken nights in the Robin Hood about how best to achieve this. Finally, it was decided that the opening music would be a Sicilian-style funeral march and that I would be carried onto the stage in a coffin by several sombre gangsters. I would then kick off the coffin lid and spring out to the surprise of an unsuspecting audience.

The lady responsible for props (theatrical properties) was horrified at our plan and let it be known that under no circumstances would she go around the town asking to borrow a coffin. We were duly stymied until cast member and well-known local hairdresser Mike Tovey found one for us. Now how he did it or where it came from I have never ascertained but, suffice it to say, it had some disturbing signs of having already served its intended purpose.

We were at a Thursday night rehearsal when he arrived all bright and breezy, flushed with success and asked if we could give him a hand with the coffin. Setting it down in Rainow Institute (our theatre) a crowd of female cast members gathered together and gazed with horror at the now open coffin.

"Surely you're not getting inside there are you Vic?" asked one of our incredulous dancers clearly filled with revulsion.

"Yes ... er ... well ... I er ..." I stammered uncertainly.

"Course he is. He's not a wimp," chimed one of the guys.

"He's the compère for God's sake," the other men added.

"Vic's an ex-pro — he's done all this stuff before."

"What? He's been a professional coffin tester?"

Against all my better judgement, I climbed into the box.

"See nothing to it," added Mr Tovey, a mite more cheerfully than I felt. I lowered myself in and, frozen with apprehension, I lay perfectly still in the dank box. To my total horror, Mike began to nail down the lid. I sprung from the coffin like a striking adder. "What the hell are you doing?" I yelled, pinning him by his throat to a nearby wall.

"I'm just tacking you in."

"Tacking me in? Tacking me in? Have you any idea what it feels like to be nailed into a second-hand coffin by a demented hairdresser humming the Sicilian Funeral March?"

At this point other cast members intervened and we adjourned to the Robin Hood for a Team Talk where it was decided to postpone any further incarcerations until the Dress Rehearsal on the following Sunday.

Understandably, we had been refused permission to leave the coffin in Rainow Institute so, on leaving the pub, Mike asked nonchalantly, "Where's it going then?"

"Where's what going?" responded our star female singer.

"The coffin, who's taking the coffin?" I snapped, still somewhat shaken by my entombment. A look of horror spread across the entire cast.

"I can't take it home."

"Well, don't ask me."

"Marion can take it."

"You can sod off."

"I can't just walk into our house and ask the baby sitter to give me a hand with a coffin." were typical responses. To everyone's relief, Mike simply said that he would take it home.

At the dress rehearsal the following Sunday afternoon, we were standing outside the Institute waiting for someone to arrive with the door key when we spotted a huge convoy of cars winding their way towards the village. There, right at the front, was Mike driving sedately along with a coffin strapped to his roof rack. No one wanted to overtake him.

"What are you doing with that thing on your roof," someone yelled from a passing car. "Is it a funeral?"

"No mate," shouted Mike in his usual good-natured way, "it's a present for the wife."

When our dress rehearsal finally got under way I was slowly coaxed back into the coffin. As the lid was closed I had a panic attack and had to be let out.

"What is it now?" asked an unsympathetic actor.

"There's no air inside there," I gasped.

"What do you expect for Christ's sake — it's a coffin," he yelled, exasperated by my timidity.

"It's not exactly a design fault is it?" added some smart Alec from the back.

"Yeah, when did you last hear of anyone returning a coffin because it was airtight? Let's just get on with it."

We agreed to time my entrance so that I was carried from the back of the Institute by six mobsters all dressed in double breasted suits, Fedora hats and spats, through the audience to the stage, where they would lay the coffin and I would spring out to everyone's utter surprise.

Forty seconds in the coffin was tolerable. A minute and I was starting to struggle. Seventy-five seconds I was gasping. Ninety seconds tops and I had to be out of that box. We rehearsed it over and over again and never went over fifty seconds.

The big night arrived and the House was packed. The bar was doing great business and everyone seemed out to have a good time. So far, so good. Outside the Institute in the snow I was getting ready for my dramatic entrance. The boys helped me into the coffin and, getting into his Sicillian role, Mike kissed me on both cheeks and crossed himself. I heard the start of the funeral march and inhaled my final breath of fresh air before the lid was nailed down.

"Right — go now!" I hollered from inside the cask. The Boys heaved me onto their shoulders.

"Hey he's farting inside there," complained one of my pallbearers.

"Phew! You're right, he is farting," said the guy at the bottom left-hand corner. They all agreed that I was indeed passing wind and unceremoniously dumped me back in the snow while they debated just how airtight it could be if they could detect my flatulence.

"Will you get a move on," I commanded, already gasping for unfarted air. Still protesting they reclaimed me and made their grand entrance, a very impressive slow march in time to the sombre music.

I heard the gasps of a stunned audience. It was all going to plan, I could afford to relax a little. As we made our way solemnly through the rows of tables and chairs, a man carrying a large camera sprang from the crowd. "Excuse me gentlemen," I vaguely heard him say, "I'm the photographer from the Macclesfield Express – could you just stop for a picture?"

Inside I was urging them to push him out of the way and deliver me onto the stage. I could not believe it when I heard them reply "Oh yeah, sure mate – where do you want us?"

Here was I nailed inside a used coffin and these stage-struck braggarts wanted to pose for press photographs.

"Just place the coffin down on the floor and all put one foot on it," he directed.

I had no idea how much time had elapsed but I was really starting to panic.

"Now if you could place your Fedora hats on the casket."

I decided there and then that I was going to die. Murdered by the insatiable needs of a Macclesfield Express photographer and the selfish preening of amateur thespians. I began to kick and yell but to no avail. The photo-shoot continued and, just when I thought that my lungs were about to explode, I smashed through the lid with such force that it splintered six foot into the air. There I was on stage like a demonic ghoul, screaming blue murder, eyes bulging, neck veins protruding, black eye make-up streaming down my face.

The audience went crazy at my dramatic entrance and stood up to express their appreciation, which continued for a good two minutes. Cameras flashed everywhere, the Macclesfield Express man was at the forefront shooting off shot after shot. I was a success, a star and waited with eager anticipation for the next edition of the Macclesfield Express.

Seven o'clock, Wednesday morning, I was down at the newsagents demanding my copy. Pulse racing I flicked through the pages and there on page seven was a large photo of the Dancing Girls with the headline 'Flappers Steal Rainow Show'. Not a single picture of my near out-of-body experience. Nothing! I leafed through the newspaper again and again in case I had missed it but I never got a mention. Was this anonymity what I had almost laid down my life for?

As soon as the Express office was open I harangued our photographer. "What happened to all those shots you took of me exploding from the coffin?" I demanded.

"Tits and bums mate." he offered by way of explanation.

"Tits and what?" I stammered.

"Tits and bums – it sells newspapers, always has."

"What?"

"We did the girls instead."

"You had me almost suffocated and 'tits and bums' was all you wanted?" I bellowed. "What about all those fantastic shots you took of the guys carrying the coffin?"

"No offence mate but half our readership are only one step away from a coffin. Those pictures would have frightened 'em to death. Tits and bums mate, tits and bums."

All Fall Down!

My disappointment with the Macclesfield Express was short-lived. The first Rainow Cabaret was generally acknowledged as a great success and so we planned another one the following year.

We were determined to improve on our initial offering and the dancing girls went to a secret hideout where they rehearsed and rehearsed two seductive numbers. Costumes were purchased, professional make up acquired and glamorous wigs obtained.

News of our intended show was spreading and we had a constant trickle of new recruits to the cause, one of whom was a robust lady of muscular thighs and little rhythm who insisted on being a dancer. I was persuaded to give a local youth, with aspirations to be an electrical engineer, the responsibility for stage lighting. He designed and reconfigured it with great imagination and enthusiasm – even if he was the only one who knew how to operate it.

Come cabaret time, the dancers had rehearsed their routine a thousand times and were determined to impress so it was decided to let them open the show. There was a buzz of anticipation as the music struck up, the curtain opened and seven highly decorative dancers standing in line like the Tiller girls began their routine to massive applause from an inebriated but appreciative audience.

As a precautionary measure, our lady of enormous thighs was placed at the end of the line but as the girls can-canned across the front of the stage she was clearly out of step. In an attempt to synchronise her efforts, she accidentally swung an enormous kick into the buttock of the girl next to her. This flung her across the stage into her neighbour, who cannoned into the one adjacent to her – and down they all went, one at a time, like a Mexican Wave, legs-akimbo, wigs flying all over the floor. Some smart Alec sitting right at the back shouted "Strike!"

The audience thought it was hilarious but the atmosphere in the girls' dressing room was dire. Still they had another dance to come in the second half, in which to redeem themselves. From there on, it went pretty much as planned despite a tendency on behalf of the audience to take over the show at every possible opportunity.

By the interval, the bar was crowded and it needed a lot longer than the allotted twenty minutes to get everyone settled down again. In spite of my

The dancing girls of Rainow

alcohol ban, some of the cast looked suspiciously tipsy and most of the audience were paralytic.

I opened the second half with a few stories and impressions while the dancers gathered themselves in the wings for their Big Number from which Thunder-Thighs had fortunately been excluded. I made the introduction, the taped music began and the dancers commenced their sensational routine which was to be lit by multicoloured spotlights — but they were not turned on! I indicated for our young stage manager to illuminate the stage and realised to my horror that he was slumped in the wings, surrounded by empty beer cans, drunk as a skunk.

I hurried off stage and grabbed him by the throat. "Throw the switch for the spotlights!" I yelled and he grabbed wildly at the handle of the control box and ripped the whole thing from the wall as he slid back down. The dancers were forced to complete their Big Number in total darkness, lit only by sparks and flashes from ripped cables and wires. While the audience could hear something was happening on stage, they didn't know precisely what.

The girls came off stage in a seething, venomous mass and I was glad my compère's role kept me permanently on stage and away from the downstairs dressing room where I could hear voices screaming for retribution. Mysteriously our young electrician disappeared during the remainder of the show and I never saw him again after that night? I'm still afraid to speculate about what might have become of him.

Enter 'Corky'

The Rainow Cabaret became an established annual event and several years later I wanted the opportunity to enjoy the show myself as a carefree member of the audience unencumbered by the responsibilities of compère. I asked for volunteers to replace me but without success until one November evening when a small, comical-looking, curly red-headed guy known to everyone at work as 'Corky' came to my office and offered his services. He was five-feet tall with a cheeky smile, crooked teeth and a reputation for combining hard work with unmitigated disaster.

He was more often the object of fun than the purveyor and despite his happy-go-lucky style, calamity was never far from his door.

"But Corky," I began "I never knew you had aspirations to join a drama group."

"Drama, me, you must be joking. I work most weekends compèring down at the Irish Club in Salford. It sounded like you needed a replacement so here I am."

It wasn't an ideal CV, but I was desperate and so, against the wishes of our deeply religious chairlady, I recruited him. I schooled him for hours in the different approach needed between a local village audience and a raucous Salford hostelry and he took it all in without protest. I reassured our chairlady that she would not be disgraced by his presence — and Corky's sunny disposition and easy-going, agreeable manner helped considerably.

On the night of the show I stood next to her at the back of the Institute smiling as she welcomed the vicar and his wife. As usual, when the show started the audience got a little boisterous and began to heckle the cast. My usual way of dealing with this was to intervene and point out that as I had the microphone and they didn't, they were better to keep quiet and I passed on this pearl of acquired wisdom to our new compère. Something, however, must have got lost in the interpretation. A loud gentleman sitting not far from the vicar continually interrupted Corky, who leapt from the stage, microphone in hand, and threatened to "stick it where the sun don't shine."

The dam had been breached. From thereon, things deteriorated rapidly and Corky's presentation reverted back to its Salford origins resplendent in four-letter words and sexual innuendo of the most unsavoury kind.

Men in the audience who dared laugh were admonished by their disgusted wives, others simply glazed over and pretended they didn't understand. Several ladies found an urgent need to use the toilet and bolted. The evening was turning into a nightmare and in answer to an emergency call I raced to give our outraged chairlady brandy and hot sweet tea in order to prevent a seizure.

At the interval she pleaded for me to replace Corky and compère the rest of the show myself but I had nothing rehearsed and so I cornered him in the dressing room.

"So what do you think so far boss?" he asked cheerfully, pint of lager in hand. I carefully explained the situation to him, taking care to spell out our chairlady's predicament.

"Oh right," he responded happily. "You should have said that the vicar and his wife were here and I'd have toned it down. Don't want to embarrass anyone."

I was mightily relieved at his compliance.

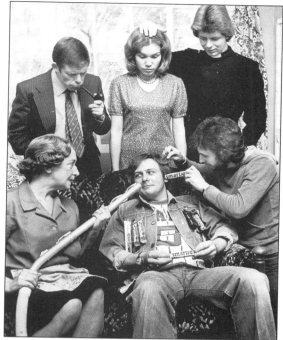

VB in Thespian days: far right, with beard

"So no dirty jokes in the second half, eh Corky?"

"No problem Vic, leave it to me, I'll not let you down."

I went back and reported the good news to our semi-delirious chairlady and she made something of a weak recovery.

The dancing girls got the second half off to a cracking start and then it was Corky's turn to introduce the following acts. I felt reasonably relaxed he was going to come good for us as he'd promised and then suddenly ... before me, centre stage, he appeared in a full nun's habit. My pulse rate rocketed and with my blood pressure hovering somewhere around Mayday, he began to explain to the audience.

"We've had to make some changes in the second half. We were going to have a bunch of naked women mud wrestling followed by a hot pot supper but the vicar is here and he's not too keen on hot pot!"

At this point, our chairlady ran downstairs sobbing and locked herself in the toilet, mercifully never to hear his next joke. The audience looked like they had all been pole-axed and I admit that my nerve went. I slid silently out of the rear door to seek sanctuary in the Robin Hood pub, where I hoped to disassociate myself from an apoplectic vicar, a dead chairlady, a compère from hell and a microphone lodged somewhere within the anatomy of an unfortunate heckler.

For months afterwards I had nightmares of this horrific experience being marketed as a party game ... "I think it was Corky in the Ladies Toilet with a microphone!"

I'm in Charge!

It's wonderful that people have such a diversity of skills. Some are artistically inclined while others can do DIY like they were born to it. Generally speaking, for such ability there is usually a balancing inability: good artists are often useless with figures while mathematicians find creative drawing and painting all but impossible.

In my case the 'inability' is very evident but attempts to identify the balancing 'skill' has so far eluded me. In any difficult situation, I can be relied upon to make it worse and any good deed I carry out is almost guaranteed to poleaxe the recipient.

So it was against this unfortunate background that my wife went into hospital one summer, leaving me to 'look after the house' and ordered me 'not to do anything embarrassing'. I adored being a young dad (I'm a still a kid at heart) and decided to take Julian, our five-year-old son, to Rainow Summer Fête .' The sun shone brightly, my son was excited about our outing. Our cup of joy 'runneth over' – nothing could blight our day.

My oldest pal Ashy was single and had phoned me to say that he would like to come over for the weekend and was it OK to bring his new dog, Oskar. He was a mate, the Best Man at my wedding, how could I refuse?

My son had expressed a desire to enter the children's fancy dress competition at the fête but without my wife's creative skills I was a bit stumped as to how to dress him up. We crawled in the loft together to rummage around and he was taken with an old set of African spears tied to a rhinoceros hide shield I had bought from a junk shop years back. A spark of genius hit me ... he could go as an African Chief. Brilliant thinking Barlow!

I spent all morning grinding the rust off the spears. I then went to work on Julian, covering him with gravy browning and making him a black curly wig out of an old tea cosy (all very non-PC). Off we went to the fête, certain we would pick up the first prize.

Just as we were leaving, Ashy duly arrived with the biggest Old English Sheepdog I had ever seen.

"You're late mate, we're just off to the fête," I informed him.

"I'll come with you," he replied.

"But the dog ... ?"

"Oh, don't worry – I'll leave him in the house, he'll be fine."

Hurriedly we settled the gigantic canine in the kitchen with an adequate supply of water and went off to collect our prize.

About an hour later and unbeknown to me, my mother decided to call in to check on the condition of the house for my wife's impending return. She made it only as far as the lounge when Oskar came hurtling through the kitchen door and pinned her to the wall. My mother was terrified of all animals and once had to be shot with a tranquilliser gun after I came home with a tortoise!

Meanwhile, the fancy dress parade was won not by an African Chief with a full set of razor-sharp spears but a dainty little angel of a girl with blond ringlets. Bo Peep had beaten us. We were mortified. By way of compensation, I promised my son a trip to the Majestic to see Jungle Book and he toddled back home happy as Larry, his little gravy-browned hand in mine.

"Look dad!" he shouted as we neared home, "there's grandma in our house."

What was going on? My mother was staggering from the house, supported between neighbours.

"It was huge! Huge! And ... and ... covered in long shaggy fur ..."

"Don't be daft mum," I reasoned. "It's only Ashy's dog, Oskar. He's not going to hurt you."

"He's not going to do anything," yelled Ashy, racing around the empty house. "He's done a runner. She's only gone and let him out!"

"As big as a Yeti," she screamed dramatically.

"Dad, when are we going to see Jungle Book?"

"Soon as you've washed that stuff off your skin," I replied, dismissing him to the bathroom.

"Why didn't you say your mother was going to be snooping around the house?" my angry pal demanded.

"Because I didn't know, you prat!" I snapped back, trying to pacify my mother currently wailing like an Iranian widow. "Look, you take care of my mum while I go and check how Julian is getting on in the bathroom."

I flew upstairs to find a bath full of greasy beige water and a sobbing figure sat in the midst of it, skin red all over from rubbing.

"It won't come off dad," he cried trying to be brave behind the tears.

"Of course it will, no problem," I said with more confidence than I felt and began to scrub his skin with the nail brush. Nothing. The damned stuff was indelible. He started to scream in pain as I applied more 'elbow grease'.

"Stop it, you're hurting me, dad," he yelled, loud enough for the whole of Rainow to hear.

"I can't find Oskar anywhere."

"Dad I'm cold."

"Keep that werewolf away from my grandson," cried my mother, bolting up the stairs

"Dad, can I get dressed."

"It had enormous fangs."

I looked from mother to son and back again, certain that I was going to wake up from a terrible nightmare when Ashy shouted from dowstairs "Hey, Vic come down here quick and have a look at this."

"Now what?" I bellowed, taking the stairs two at a time.

"Look at that smoke," he pointed towards the lounge carpet.

Sure enough, there was a light smog seeping through the floor. It was a hot summer's day, and we had no fire burning. Other than it being a new underground station, I had no idea of the cause. I decided to seek advice from the fire brigade and made a phone call without going through the emergency service number.

"Hello, my name's Vic Barlow and I live at ... ... We've got a bit of smoke in the lounge and I was just wondering if you could possibly ask one of your chaps to maybe call in on his way home from work and offer some advice. No mad urgency, just if he's passing." I was told that 'a chap' would be with me shortly and, suitably reassured, I returned to the bathroom where my mother was drying her now shivering grandson and muttering, "The Lord is my shepherd," beneath her breath.

To my horror the bath looked like a huge bowl of insipid gravy while my son was now a hideous patchwork of brown and white. I was just considering whether I should kill my best pal or myself, when a fire engine arrived, siren wailing, lights flashing and a larger group of neighbours began to gather around outside. This was precisely what I didn't want. I was rushing up the drive to explain to the Chief Fire Officer that such a display of manpower was unnecessary when a second engine appeared accompanied by a police car, both with sirens screaming.

Team Number Two jumped down from the engine and brushed past me purposefully, radios squawking and met up with the first team who to my a utter amazement had already axed through the lounge floor carpet.

"Excuse me officer," I protested.

"Stand back, sir." Whack! and another chunk of floor board disintegrated under the axe.

He then ordered everyone out of the house and we stood on the drive in a bewildered state surrounded by emergency vehicles and nosy neighbours while firemen threw armsful of smoking floorboards and carpet onto the front lawn.

"There's your problem," shouted the Chief Fire Officer and held aloft a large section of glowing wooden floor joist. "Leave that for a few more hours and whoooosh!" He made a gesture which indicated dire consequences.

"Who fitted that fireplace?" he asked in the manner in which a new hair-dresser always asks "Who did your hair last?"

"Err ... the builder I suppose," I responded.

"Well he should be locked up. He ran the flooring joist right into your ash pan. It's been drying out and heating up for years. It was just ready to combust. Could have roasted the lot of you while you slept." I shuddered and hugged my son closer.

"Burnt alive and never known about it."

"Yes thank you mother, I think I've got the picture."

"Unrecognisable except for your teeth."

"Mother, will you be quiet."

"And your jewellery."

"That's enough."

"Cremated in your own beds."

"For Christ's sake mother, belt up!" I screamed and the whole street stood back and gasped. At this precise point, Ashy's dog came bounding down the drive."That's it, that's it!" screeched my mother, suddenly jump-ing protectively in front of my son as though Oskar was about to rip out his heart and eat it.

"Who's a good boy then?" shouted Ashy, deliriously happy at the return of his canine accomplice.

"Get rid of it. Get rid of it," screamed my mother, close to hysterics.

"Oh shut up you silly sod," responded Ashy

"Don't you call Mrs Barlow a silly sod," yelled a neighbour, inexplicably defensive of my mother, whom he had never previously met.

"I don't want to be eaten alive by that Yeti either," chipped in a small fireofficer in a uniform three sizes too big.

"Look, sod off the lot of you," I yelled unwisely to the assembled crowd made up entirely of people I was going to have to live alongside for the next decade.

"Well she is being a bit overdramatic," offered a guy from across the street.

Everyone began to argue with each other.

"She's totally ga-ga if you ask me."

"How can you say that? She's Vic's mother."

"And the grandmother of that lovely skewbald child."

"It should be under control. It's a menace."

"Don't you call my dog a menace."

"She's got a point though."

People started pushing each other. Oskar got into the spirit of things and leapt around on his hind legs, barking furiously. My mother ran screaming up the street and Ashy was threatening to thump anyone who touched his dog.

As the fire engines pulled away I withdrew from the fracas to survey the scene. The lounge had a huge hole in the middle with large chunks of splintered wood protruding, like a trap sprung in a jungle clearing by an unsuspecting elephant.

The front lawn was full of smouldering embers and bits of unravelled carpet. The bathroom looked as though it belonged to the Bisto Kid. Far from winning the fancy-dress competition our shell-shocked son looked as though he stood more chance of being 'Best in Show' at a gymkhana.

I barely heard the telephone ring. "Hi, Vic Barlow," I stammered into the phone hoping it was The Readers Digest to say that I'd been chosen for a six-month expedition up the Orinoco leaving immediately.

"Hello, remember me, your wife? I've got some good news, I've been discharged. They are bringing me home right now. Can't wait to get back. Is everything under control?"

Summer Madness

I adore Macclesfield for its many characters and Rainow, where I lived in the '70s and '80s had more than its fair share. Among others, it still has a truly amazing vicar who can not only compose music on a bare tabletop (no piano required) and perform stand-up comedy but is also a wizard with puppets. A unique combination for a vicar wouldn't you say?

During a meeting held to determine the format of the village fête, our vicar (known to all as the Rev. Les) suggested I might 'like to go into the stocks'. This involved standing for hours with my head and hands protruding through the stocks while villagers threw wet sponges at me for 10 pence a throw. Far from 'liking it' I found the prospect appalling and said so in no uncertain terms.

"Oh come on, Vic," said the Rev. Les. "It'll be great fun and it's for a good cause," he added with a beatific smile guaranteed to gain compliance. "And it won't hurt you," he added delivering the sucker punch.

"Yeah, OK put me down for the stocks then," I agreed reluctantly as the Rev. Les patted me on the back, already moving the agenda along so as to rope in his next unsuspecting victim.

Come the day, I had a severe attack of foreboding and, were it not that my commitment had been made directly to a representative of the Almighty, I would have found good reason to renege. Arriving at the school field where the fête was held, I surveyed the scene. A large marquee was in the prime central position with pony rides and smaller stalls around the perimeter. My stocks had already been erected and were standing in long grass in a remote corner certain to be missed by almost everyone. That was fine by me and I felt a lot more cheery as I stripped down to my shorts and was duly locked into position.

Rainow fell race, 1977. That's me, all in white.

I was standing there, day-dreaming in the sunshine, taking in the pleasant sounds of summer, when a tractor arrived and two hairy-chested farmers unloaded several large barrels, together with a canvas awning.

"So what's going on here then?" I asked inquisitively.

"Beer tent, mate."

"You what?"

"Beer tent, can't have a summer fête with no beer tent."

"Yeah, right but you can't put it here," I directed wiggling my fingers to indicate the exact location where erection should not take place.

"Is that so?" they replied, erecting even as they spoke.

I knew this meant trouble. Beer was the time-honoured drink of men; such women as imbibed were of the Ma Larkin type, i.e. robust in health and stout of countenance. Perfeck!

I had been sold on the idea of standing in the stocks by images of elderly ladies in summer frocks and quaint hats counting out their ten pence from little leather purses, barely able to lift a wet sponge, never mind throw one. This was not going to plan.

The first hour was fairly quiet and, other than cramp, I suffered no great discomfort from the one or two children that had flung sponges at me while awaiting a vacant pony.

Mid-afternoon and the tide began to change as more and more men decided to quench their thirst.

"Eh fellas, tek a look at this," shouted a thickset neighbour to a small group of drinkers standing beside the beer tent. "It's Vic Barlow in the stocks."

They ambled over, beer in hand.

"Bet you can't smack him square in the face."

"Quid says I can."

"Quid says you can't." They were talking as if I couldn't hear.

"Put me down for a quid as well."

"Yeah, and me."

"Right you're on, the lot of you, even money."

I didn't like the sound of this one little bit.

The first sponge hurtled towards me and passed six inches over my head.

"Best out of three," yelled the aggravated punter.

"Sod off, you missed."

"I'll put another quid down then."

"Eh, get to the back of the queue – you've had your go."

Another laden sponge whistled towards me and hit the stocks.

"Like taking candy from a baby," proclaimed the enriched bookmaker.

I was absorbed in the banter when another aquatic missile caught me by surprise smack in the face. The shockwaves went right down my body. The vicar had somehow failed to mention that in his long experience of village fêtes, a wet sponge hurled from twelve feet has exactly the same impact as a Cheshire brick.

No sooner had I regained some sort of composure than I received another direct hit and I began to panic. I felt like I was drowning in a heavy sea and being bodily battered by debris. Smack! Another direct hit. Right that was it, I'd had enough and I spotted the vicar passing by.

"Vicar," I screamed, "can I have a word?"

"Ah, four pounds already," he smiled examining the biscuit tin into which my tormentors paid their money. "Keep up the good work." And with that, he disappeared into the crowd.

I couldn't think what word in Collins English Dictionary meant 'the murder of clergy' but I was definitely going to look it up as soon as I got out.

I had been the writer of Rainow Players Cabaret for many years and had used this forum for publicly taking the Mickey out of local characters who, in the main, had always taken the ridicule in good part, or so I thought.

I was languishing in the stocks towards the end of the day, sustained only by consideration of the various ways in which to eliminate a vicar when I heard the unmistakable laugh of Billy Moss, local farmer and a prime target of my theatrical satire.

"Well, well, look who we've got here," he exclaimed with a blood chilling toothy grin like one of those hillbillies in 'Deliverance'.

"How much?" he inquired of the dear old lady taking the money on my behalf.

"Ten pence a sponge, Billy," she replied in total innocence.

A crowd began to gather as word spread that Billy was out to seek revenge

"Right, give us a quid's worth."

A pound was a lot of sponges and I wondered if he had decided to treat the little kids around him to a free throw.

"What was it you said about me and my fondness for sheep?" he asked rolling up his sleeves.

"Nothing really Billy — it was just a stupid joke that's all."

"Oh a joke was it? A joke? Well try this for a joke!" and a sponge the weight of a cannon ball hit me smack in the face.

"You've broken my sodding nose you idiot," I screamed in terror.

"Oh well, best I don't aim for it any more then," he chortled menacingly and hurled another shot straight into my groin.

The pain was excruciating and my limp body slid into the pole like the object of a Colombian firing squad. I am told that many people undergoing torture find that the brain switches off as part of their defence mechanism. And so it was with me as I slipped into a surreal world of swirling Macclesfield Express headlines proclaiming 'Rainow Man Maimed In Sponge Attack! Local Vicar Falls Victim To Acid Bath Killer! Acid Bath Killer Loses Arm Pulling Plug Out! ...'

Never Trust a Vicar

The vicar also played a large part in the annual village cabaret where he would regale us with a collection of jokes much to everyone's great amusement, especially that of his wife, and he usually rounded off his performance with a piano recital.

He always wore his clerical collar and I cannot recount the number of times a member of the audience from outside the village would comment "That guy dressed up as a vicar was brilliant!" Unlike the rest of the cast, whom I rehearsed mercilessly for eight weeks beforehand, the vicar was excused rehearsals on the grounds of his commitment to a Greater Authority and turned up merely for the show itself. To avoid embarrassment, his 'representatives' in the shape of various members of the church committee did attend dress rehearsals on his behalf to ensure nothing of an 'unsuitable' nature would be performed that might impugn his reputation.

As producer of this theatrical extravaganza I was unable to take part in any of the sketches I had written but, being a 'stage-struck' individual, I always did a stand-up routine to satisfy my craving for applause.

Following a Sunday dress rehearsal before one particular cabaret, a church lady who had been taking copious notes approached me with an expression of foreboding.

"Your material is hardly suitable for an audience that includes the vicar and his wife," she said gravely.

"It's all I've got. It's a bit late to find new material now."

"No, no it will never do," she continued as though I hadn't spoken.

"But I've been rehearsing for eight weeks, that's the best routine I've ever written." I protested.

"No not suitable at all."

"Why, what's wrong?" I demanded to know.

"Two nuns and a skinhead." she said pointedly tapping her pencil on her notepad, "most unseemly."

"OK I'll cut the nuns joke."

"And the bishop in the bath?" she raised her eyebrows accusingly.

"All right I'll cut that too."

In the end I cut out three-quarters of my act and went home to burn the midnight oil and dig out as much replacement stuff as I could find from old scripts. I wrote and rewrote my routine and was determined to 'knock 'em dead'.

Come show time I bounced onto the stage and gave it my best shot but the audience looked like they had all been drinking Blue Circle and sat through my entire act in stony silence. When I finally finished, the sparse applause suggested that they were all handcuffed together. Obviously, they were not in the mood for stand-up comedy. I pitied the vicar having to endure this.

The dancing girls livened things up considerably in the second half and after a couple of well-received sketches I introduced the vicar, retiring to the wings and hardly able to watch him die the same slow death as me. He ambled on to the stage in his usual diffident manner and began his routine. "There were two nuns and a skinhead on the bus" ... He told the joke, my joke. The audience went wild. He followed it with, "A bishop was sitting in the bath counting his legs." The audience loved it. In the next twenty minutes, he performed my entire routine, the one I had been rehearsing for eight weeks. He was a huge success. They wouldn't let him leave the stage. I couldn't believe it. I'd been duped. Suckered by an old biddy from the parish church and a stage-struck vicar.

Part 2: Expressing Myself

My letters published in the Macc Express were the springboard for 'Macclesfield Exposed!' so it's only fitting that I include some of those from recent years that started the ball rolling. Remember these?

---

23 January 1997

Dear Sir,

GET OUT OF TOWN!

What dark forces are at work in our town for an ordinary law abiding resident to be put in fear of the lives of his family by simply exercising his democratic right to be part of a local Planning Action Group? Although I have no personal interest in this group I think everyone in our area should be alarmed to learn that Mr Paul McMahon has been receiving death threats from a group of people with sufficient funds to enable them to maintain an ongoing surveillance of this man and his children. It would appear that for his own part Mr McMahon is fighting over the sale of land in the green belt, surely a topic of great concern to us all.

We must scrutinise all powerful individuals, organisations or companies that stand to gain by terrorising Mr McMahon and his Planning Action Group. If we, as a community, accept that one of our residents can be frightened into selling up and leaving the area for simply challenging the planning decisions of our town how long will it be before the tentacles of fear and intimidation reach out and touch all of us?

There could be no better issue for our forthright MP, Mr Winterton, to involve himself in. He would undoubtedly be the first person to want to ensure that those parties with an interest in developing land in and around Macclesfield would not profit by exerting undue influence. I think we should all stand squarely behind Mr McMahon and his family and let it be known that threats and intimidation will not be tolerated in Macclesfield.

I thank the Express for alerting us to this evil and would urge you to put all further developments on the front page.

Yours faithfully,

V. Barlow

10 February 1997

This was a little piece I wrote in response to Nick Winterton's reaction to the Macclesfield Express's support of Wizard Radio when the local Radio Franchise was being decided upon.

Dear Sir,

RADIO WARS

Regardless of your political persuasion I am sure you will agree that Nick Winterton is without doubt one of the more conscientious Members of Parliament. He opens things, closes things, rails against things, proposes things. He is, it has to be said, a great doer of 'things'.

There are critically ill patients unable to find hospital beds, old-age pensioners struggling to survive on an income insufficient to feed a gerbil, and the unrelenting onslaught of the drug culture upon our precious children all clamouring for attention. One wonders how any human being, no matter how conscientious, can decide which issues to champion.

It came therefore as something of a surprise to find that out of this plethora of human misery the Macclesfield Express article on Wizard Radio has so incurred his wrath that it has risen to the top of his agenda. He was apparently 'appalled' at the 'gross abuse of editorial impartiality'.

He may have a point. It may have been presumptuous in its implication that Wizard would win the much-coveted Local Radio Franchise. It may also be that, as long as we have a good local radio station, free of Chris Evans, generally speaking the rest of us don't give a toss.

The point is, Nick, that whilst we all have aged friends and relatives to worry about, and our children's health and welfare over which to agonise, we are, regrettably, indifferent to the name of Radio Whatever. It is, I admit, possible that in a Christmas yet to come some homeless unfortunate languishing in a frozen Chestergate may be so incensed by hearing Wizard Radio emanating from a passing vehicle that he forgoes the succour and comfort afforded him by the doorway of Russell Kellar's excellent establishment and, adorned only in a sandwich board, disappears towards Mill Street screaming 'Impartiality in Local Radio Licensing'. It is possible ... but probably not in our lifetime.

Priorities Nick, priorities.

Yours faithfully,

Vic Barlow

15 June 1997

Dear Sir,

A PLAYTIME STORY!

Can anyone blame the parents and children from the Victoria Road area for wanting to retain one of the few remaining green fields for playing in their area (Macclesfield Express lead story). During the eighties we were taught that 'greed is good' and our children have been paying the price ever since. In Poynton the only major play area for the local children has always been the large field alongside the High School where generations of youngsters have flown kites, played football and wandered around completely safe from the dangers of growing traffic.

Three years ago the Education Authority were refused planning permission and were unable to sell it for housing development. Despite the obvious risk of vandalism school perimeter fences were, and still are, left rotting and trampled while an all-encompassing State of the Art fence was erected around the entire playing field. The result is that children are now forced to play on the streets and roads.

The significant cost of this operation took place against a background of severe budgetary cuts and one can only assume it was either a calculated act of spite or in order to reduce the number of objections next time a planning application is made. If councils can make compulsory purchase orders on private homes, why not do the same on precious local land to enable our children to play in safety?

Your faithfully,

Vic Barlow

---

26 July 1997

Dear Sir,

IN THE HEAT OF THE NIGHT

Let me be the first to congratulate B&Q for their public-spirited action in cutting down the fifty-year-old trees obscuring the public view of their beautiful store, and so thoughtful of them to do it in the dead of night when no-one was around.

Only recently my ears were affronted by a song thrush in one of those accursed trees, totally spoiling my enjoyment of the Chemical Brothers emanating from a thoughtfully placed radio behind the ketchup dispenser on the nearby hot-dog stand. No doubt, B&Q will know exactly how to deal with this piece of flying flotsam, should it have the temerity to return.

I, for one, am sick and tired of having my view of retail parks and industrial estates obstructed by trees, plants and feathered impedimenta. Surely, B&Q have proved to us all that there is an answer and that we need not put up with this one moment longer. Thank you B&Q. We will all rest more easily in each others' beds knowing that, whilst we are sleeping, you are out there ridding us of superfluous foliage.

Yours faithfully,

Vic Barlow

---

19 September 1997

Dear Sir,

AN OPEN AND SHUT CASE!

The vast amount of police and Court time spent since 1989 on repeatedly prosecuting that Criminal Mastermind Tim Hudson for his sinister construction of two unsightly gates at Birtles Hall is a major stroke in our local War against Crime.

The message must be clear now to every thief, burglar, rapist and violent offender: 'We may not have the manpower or resources to prevent you from perpetrating your evil activities but let there be no doubt a line has been drawn from which we shall not retreat. Should any one of your number have the depravity to build a large set of wrought iron gates (without planning permission) the full force of the Macclesfield Law Enforcement Agencies will be down upon you like a ton of bricks.'

That is, of course, always assuming you are not Tesco or Sainsbury – in which case we welcome your innovative idea and insist on building you your own dual carriageway with a roundabout sited in the appropriate position.

Yours faithfully,

Vic Barlow

6 December 1997

Dear Sir,

CHRISTMAS CRACKERS!

Reading through the back issues of the Macclesfield Express it makes me realise how lucky we all are to live in such a unique and humorous town. We have, in the past had the fabulous story of the Macclesfield Forest Deer where it was suggested that the best way to stop the deer ripping bark off the trees was to cover the tree base in lion dung! Brilliant lateral thinking, were it not for the fact that there are over a million trees in Macclesfield Forest and the only lions within a thirty mile radius are two geriatric males at Chester Zoo. Still I suppose we could have fed them syrup of figs.

Then we had the amazing story of the four midwives' uniforms stolen from a car. Police uniforms you can understand, security officers maybe – but what sort of job were they planning to pull dressed as a gang of midwives? Were they likely to burst into Mothercare yelling, "OK, this is a Caesarean – lie on your back with your legs in the air and no-one will get hurt."

With masterful irony just as the plight of the homeless in Macclesfield was becoming a serious issue ... lo and behold, £100,000 of lottery money goes to Prestbury Tennis Club for floodlighting. No doubt if the poor unfortunates sleeping in Macclesfield doorways this Christmas nip down to Prestbury, they will at least be able to warm up with a set of doubles.

I loved the story about the Ladies Barber-Shop Quartet who were looking for additional members as there numbers had shrunk to 'around forty'.

But best of all has to he the stunning idea of an Open Day at Macclesfield Crematorium. Is that the most brilliant idea or what? This is definitely going to put Macclesfield in its rightful place at the very top of every comedian's repertoire.

So, when you examine the facts, it's little wonder that Macclesfield Hospital has for years been one of the country's major centres for the treatment of depression. All they ever had to do was give patients a copy of the Macclesfield Express and let them have a read. Personally, I think the Council should introduce a 'Tickle Tax' payable by any residents new to the borough who look in dire need of a good laugh.

Isn't life wonderful?

Merry Christmas Macclesfield.

Vic Barlow

24 February 1998

Dear Sir,

IN SAFE HANDS?

Macclesfield, I love you! Where else in this country would you find a competition won by a courageous woman with a life-long fear of water who was prepared to jump in to the deep end of the local swimming pool on the understanding that she would be rescued by the town's star footballer (Macclesfield Express Feb. 22nd) – only to find that the proposed lifeguard was the only athlete on the face of the planet who couldn't swim. It's just brilliant! I worked in Ireland for twenty years but Maxonians make the Irish look like the entire membership of Mensa.

The really exciting thing about Macclesfield is that *anything* is possible. Can't you just see future front pages of the Macclesfield Express ... 'Sammy McIlroy signs Stevie Wonder as new goalkeeper' ... 'New Macclesfield Mul-

tiplex Cinema Opens ... in Leek' ... 'Jones Homes donate development land free for use as playing field.' (Well, maybe not EVERYTHING is possible.)

Yours faithfully,

Vic Barlow

2 April 1998

Dear Sir,

DRINK OR DIE!

Isn't it wonderful to know that the Majestic Cinema will be replaced by a massive new Public House? Many is the time my friends and I leave the White Lion and have to slog all the way up to The Filigree and Firkin without any refreshment, a journey of almost *fifty* yards (and all up-hill).

Dehydration can be a major problem and it amazes me that we have not had more fatalities in the hot summer months when this unforgiving climb can take ... almost a minute! It's also comforting to know that the type of hostelry planned will be specifically aimed at the young drinker. (The same group currently having drinking lessons in Prestbury?)

How pleasant it will be to walk down Mill Street on a balmy summer evening and see dozens of inebriated teenagers spilling out onto the pavements. It will further enhance our image as a jolly top-notch place to have a trouble-free night out with one's family. Those Doubting Thomas's who believe that it will make Mill Street into a noisy, yobbish, place to be avoided after dark have simply forgotten what good Accident and Emergency facilities we have in Macclesfield.

With only forty eight pubs in the town the need for a Super Dooper, Giant Size Boozer is obvious. At the moment, it's possible to walk for yards without ever seeing a pub. So, good luck to all concerned. Another masterpiece of planning and foresight.

Yours faithfully,

Vic Barlow

31 May 1998

Dear Sir,

JUST ASK MACC!

Why, Oh Why, do we in Macclesfield always have to show the way to the rest of the country in almost every field of activity? When people throughout Britain were worrying about the length of Hospital Waiting Lists, Macclesfield didn't waste time complaining. We swung into action and knocked down one of our hospitals and replaced it with a Sainsbury's and from that day to this no-one has ever been waiting for more than a few minutes. Simple ideas, simple solutions.

People in Birmingham complained bitterly that a new by-pass to the M6 would increase congestion around their city. Macclesfield had to show them this need not be so by building a by-pass to Leek which, because no one actually wants to go there, has hardly increased congestion at all. Planning – that's all it takes: planning and foresight.

All of which brings me to the ubiquitous Speed Camera much loved by councils and police forces throughout Britain. The other day I was bouncing over the Ivy Road speed bumps in my car when I tuned into Silk FM to hear someone called R. Kelly singing 'I believe I can fly'. (A song I understand he had written whilst driving down Brocklehurst Way.)

"What a coincidence," I thought, as I swerved to avoid an oncoming coach travelling in the middle of the road. This is 'traffic calming' at its best I thought, as my head smashed against the windscreen during an emergency stop made to avoid hitting the bollards that are placed so as to deliberately narrow the road. But the point is it made me *concentrate*. All the speed cameras in the world won't make a driver concentrate like a cast iron bollard embedded in his bonnet or the sight of an oncoming bus running straight over his roof.

The motorways have more cameras than Brian Ollier but it doesn't stop people driving at over 100mph. Had the authorities followed Macclesfield's lead none of this would happen. Drivers flying down the outside lane would suddenly be confronted by a 'Calming' set of cast-iron bollards. The inside lane would be an ocean of speed bumps forcing motorists into the central lane where they would be met with traffic travelling in the opposite direction (as a result of 'Road Narrowing'). No one would ever speed again. Problem solved.

It's about time the rest of Britain got wise. Do it the right way, do it the only way. DO IT THE MACCLESFIELD WAY!

Yours faithfully,

Vic Barlow

12 June 1998

Dear Sir,

LABOUR PAINS!

I was fascinated by Nick Winterton's view that the Government have had a disappointing first year in office. Let's review the year from a Tory perspective.

After a crushing and humiliating defeat they elect a new leader who has all the charisma of the Lindow Peat Bog Man. Following disastrous Poll ratings for Mr Hague, he duly appoints Sebastian Coe as his special adviser. This is a man whose personal presence is on a par with the Speaking Clock – to call him wooden is an insult to Pinnoccio.

As an ex-runner myself I found Seb Coe's performance on the track truly inspirational, but his only asset to the Tory Party is his famous name. Would anyone have chosen Cyril Smith for the Olympic 800 metres on the strength of his name? I think Mr Hague might have done!

If this is a measure of Tory Party Leadership as that other famous person on Dad's Army used to say "We're all doomed".

We do love you Nick but 'Get Real'.

Yours faithfully,

Vic Barlow

14 June 1998

Dear Sir,

OUR CILLA

Am I alone in spotting the amazing resemblance between our Council Leader Mrs Margaret Duddy and that other famous public figure Cilla Black? It should have been obvious to me when, attending a recent Council Meeting I heard Mrs Duddy raise an issue with another councillor with the words "Av Gorra question fer you, Number Two." Something of a give-away, don't you think?

I have followed Mrs Duddy's public career very carefully and I have noticed that she has never on any occasion appeared together with Cilla. Considering the fact that she has met many celebrities and public figures and is an associate of Janet Jackson I thought this rather curious. I suppose the conclusive evidence came when she began her welcoming address at a recent formal dinner by announcing, "Wiv gorra lorra lovely guests."

Everyone, not withstanding their celebrity status, should be allowed some privacy but I put it to you that our Council Leader Mrs Margaret Duddy and Ms. Cilla Black are one and the same person. In the event of Mrs Duddy wishing to publicly disprove my theory I hereby challenge her to appear on the steps of Macclesfield Town Hall with Cilla by her side or, alternatively, sing three verses of "Anyone who had a Heart " live on Silk FM and let the listeners decide.

A lorra lorra luv,

Vic Barlow

---

11 August 1998

Dear Sir,

ARE WE THERE YET?

The good people of Macclesfield whom I love dearly can be inordinately stupid at times. Not long ago, they moaned and complained that they wanted more parking facilities close to the town centre shops. In actual fact, what they really needed was more healthy walking exercise (preferably loaded with heavy shopping) and, to their credit, the Council built Jordangate Car Park which is farther away from the town centre than most nuclear power plants. The enforced exercise has probably been a lifesaver for those suffering from angina.

Then there was the ludicrous suggestion that we should have a town centre by-pass that actually by-passed the town centre, when it was painfully obvious that what was required was a dual-carriageway linking up Sainsbury's with Tesco's and forming a non-moving solid wall of traffic to reduce the risks caused by speeding.

More recently we have had people demanding a multiplex cinema to be built at

...BIG PICTURE'S JUST STARTIN' IN STOCKPORT, LUV...

Lyme Green, and quite frankly I for one am sick of the short-sighted views of the Macclesfield public. Anyone with half a brain can see the shortage of suitable land for development in our borough. Therefore it behoves us to ensure that every new building project is balanced and complementary to our future needs and with dozens of cinemas available within a full days travel a cinema at Lyme green would be a waste of our precious resources. Fortunately for us the Council has recognised our stupidity and instead intends to approve the building of what our community *really* needs, an Asda supermarket.

Now imagine ... it's a rainy Saturday morning and the kids want to go and see 'The Teletubbies Slay Anastasia' or whatever the latest Disney film might be. You load them up in the car and call in at the new Lyme Green Asda for provisions for your long journey.

Now as you move at a snail's pace along London Road the only way to keep the kids quiet is to open the shopping and feed them crisps and bickies etc. By the time you get to Arighi's the supplies have already run out and the kids need to go to the toilet.

Hey Presto! You're gridlocked at Hibel Road but, within half an hour, you can crawl round to Tesco and renew your supplies, fill up with petrol, take the kids to the loo and still be in Manchester in time for the midnight show.

You see, we are like children who don't always know what they want and although not glaringly obvious you can now understand why our Council would not want us to have a cinema in Macclesfield when another supermarket is just what we need.

Yours faithfully,

Vic Barlow

---

7 November 1998

NB: This letter was written following the horrendous case of Essex Police dog handlers who were convicted of hanging one of their own dogs by its lead and then kicking it to death during a training seminar. The Inspector in charge denied responsibility stating that as he had as many as *three* officers working for him he could not possibly know what each one was doing.

Dear Sir,

IT'S A DOG'S LIFE!

I write to you full of excitement – I have just seen the first-ever police constable on foot in Sutton! I thought it must be the beginning of summer (like the first cuckoo) but no, it was definitely November and there he was large as life hopping about on the pavement looking very chirpy indeed.

I took out my binoculars to get a closer look and he didn't seem to have any particular purpose. Maybe he was an Essex Police dog handler who had just finished hanging his dog for the day and had travelled North to relax after a hard day's strangling?

To my utter astonishment he knocked on my front door and caused great panic among my own two dogs who were already kicking themselves in the stomach just to show willing. There was relief all round when I discovered he was looking for someone of whom I'd never heard.

Probably he was looking for his Inspector who denied he was in charge of police dogs in Essex or even what one does? No one had ever told him and, if they had, he was managing a team of three and could not be expected to remember what each and everyone of them did. Moreover, all the dogs were German Shepherds and he doesn't speak German.

The lone constable walked from my front door into the sunset, dogless. Heaven knows how long we shall have to wait in Sutton before we get another sighting but I have found a letter from my dogs to Santa asking for no less than suits of full body armour for Christmas – just in case!

Yours faithfully,

Vic Barlow

---

22 November 1998

Dear Sir,

THE 'GOOD PEOPLE' OF MACC

Mrs Stanier wrote from Beech Farm drive (Macclesfield Express, Nov. 18) expressing her 'disbelief' at the Borough Council Planning Committee's decision to grant permission for the building of a block of flats in the Bollin Valley, completely against the Council's own Local Plan and the Chief Planner's recommended refusal. Obviously Mrs Stanier has failed to realise that this is Macclesfield and doesn't fully understand how things work in our neck of the woods so, in the interest of goodwill to all men, please allow me to explain.

When the Council recently adopted the Local Plan which is *against* such new developments they were only thinking of the Good People of Macclesfield and when the Chief Planning Officer recommended *refusal* of this specific proposal he was also thinking only of the Good People of Macclesfield. With me so far?

Now, when the Planning Committee subsequently *approved* this specific proposal they were still thinking of the Good People of Macclesfield but *not* the same Good People of Macclesfield as they were originally thinking about when they were *against* it. Still with me?

Had the Chief Planning Officer known which Good People of Macclesfield the Planning Committee was thinking about when they were thinking about it the second time, he would not have recommended *refusal* the first time. Moreover, had the Planning Committee been thinking about the same good people of Macclesfield the second time as they were thinking about the first time then the Chief Planning Officer's decision would have concurred with their *refusal* the first time. Simple!

Secondly, Mrs Stanier asks how could the Council not know that the sports field near to the proposed development had only recently been under two feet of water when she personally had photographic evidence? Well, Mrs Stanier, I have to tell you that, in years gone by, this particular area was known as

'Tytherington Beach' and although you took your photographs when the tide was *in* the Council did not attend the site until the tide was *out*.

So, there you are – all straightforward and above board and always for the Good People of Macclesfield. If only we knew WHICH Good People!

Yours faithfully,

Vic Barlow

11 February 1999

Dear Sir,

ELEPHANTS NEVER FORGET

What an absolute superb idea to turn the Vicky Park Flats site into a Safari Park. Can you imagine the opening ceremony with Nick Winterton's photograph plastered across the front of the Macclesfield Express with his head stuck in a lion's mouth (and the rest of him inside the lion). Brilliant.

Russell Kellar will no doubt be there trying to hire out his best monkey suits to ... er ... monkeys, for when they take over the Town Hall. Alligators could be accommodated on the playing fields near Beach Farm Drive to make it easy

for the Council to recognise a flood – if they are swimming it's flooded, if they're basking it isn't.

One could sit in the pleasant surroundings of Arighi Bianchi's restaurant with a giraffe of wine and watch the orang-utans re-distribute the windscreen wipers on parked cars.

Best of all will be the bread counter at Tesco when the elephants pop over for elevenses. Make a mental note not to stand behind them at the check-out. It could take a while.

This is a truly great town. Cast-iron bollards in the middle of the road to 'calm' traffic. A by-pass that actually doesn't by-pass anywhere and leads to nowhere! A nationally respected hospital exchanged for a Sainsbury's! A multi-storey car park for shoppers situated in Jordangate where there aren't any shops! The list is endless, but a Safari Park? Even by Macclesfield standards this is entering brand gnu territory.

Fellow Maxonians arise! We are the Chosen People. We may not all be rich and famous. We may not all be solvent, but we are *all* completely ga-ga! No-one can take that away from us! It's just the way it is. Be proud, be brave and always remember ... it's a jungle out there!

Yours faithfully,

Vic Barlow

---

13 August 1999

Dear Sir,

IT'S JAMAICA, MAN!

What exactly is B. Stubbs (Letters August 1st) talking about when she suggests that the Council should re-site Macclesfield's Market from its desolate position at the far-side of Churchill Way to the bustling Market Square? Where has she been living for the past fifty years?

There is no way Macclesfield Council would ever put the Market on this place intended for ... er ... er. Wel l.. a market actually. This is the council that built Jordangate Car Park for Shoppers. A car park further away from town centre shops than most nuclear power stations. A council that constructed a by-pass for busy M6 and Potteries traffic that actually goes to Leek. The very same council that gave planning permission for houses on a flat piece of the Bollin Valley that regularly floods and holds more water than Lamaload reservoir.

My advice to Mrs Stubbs is: relax, take a chill pill, smoke. This is Macclesfield the town where a pizza can get to your house quicker than an ambulance. We are the Jamaica of Cheshire. Go with the flow man.

Vic Barlow

---

28 September 1999

Dear Sir,

'MACCLESFIELD CALLING'

Just when I thought I wasn't going to write for a while the Macclesfield Express hit me with a fantastic front page story of the councillor who dodged flying bottles on a Saturday lunchtime to report a riot right outside Macclesfield Police Station only to find it shut.

It was only recently revealed that the CCTV in the town centre is actually viewed *the day after* on videotape by police in *Wilmslow*. So, although your local police cannot stop you being beaten up they can at least rent you a nice video to show the wife and kiddies.

Which brings me to the telephone service – for, as anyone who has called Macclesfield Police will know, the call actually goes to Chester. I can see that in the not too distant future you will call the police to hear the following:

"Hello this is Macclesfield Police Station. If you have a touch-tone telephone press the star key now.

In order that your call may be correctly routed please chose one of the following options.

If you are being burgled press One.

If you are being attacked by a mad axe-man, press Two.

If you are trapped under a Bostocks' bus, press Three.

For all other life threatening situations, please press Four.

Thank you for selecting Two.

You are being attacked by a mad axe-man. You now have three choices:

If the axe-man has yet to swing his axe, press One.

If he has swung and missed press, Two

If he has already caught you a glancing blow, press Three.

Thank you. You have been caught a glancing blow. We are now putting you through ...

"Hello you have reached the 'Caught by a Glancing Blow from a Mad

Axe-Man Dept.' Unfortunately all our Officers are busy putting film in traffic cameras but will be with you shortly. Please hold while we play you some crappy music. "

Sounds a bit far fetched? You wouldn't want to bet on it.

Yours faithfully,

Vic Barlow

---

3 November 1999

Dear Sir,

THE WHOLE TRUTH AND NOTHING BUT THE TRUTH, SO HELP US!

I have just read the letter in the Macclesfield Express from Councillor Margaret Duddy regarding the quality of police work in our town. Oh Maggie, Maggie, Maggie!

Of course we all think the police do a grand job. So did the Bengal Lancers, The Ghurkas and The Queen's Royal Horse Artillery, but we don't see much of them on the streets of Macclesfield either.

It's absolutely no consolation to some poor unfortunate young man having his face re-engineered by a gang of drunks in Mill Street to know that at least it's all being recorded on video ... in Wilmslow!

Reiterating Official Policy is not what we need. Strangely enough what people actually want is for our Boys in Blue to be where we are, on the streets and when there is an incident, we would preferably like them to come out to visit us rather than us going to see them.

It's no good telling some old lady who's being terrorised by Kids From Hell that 'Our Police Station is manned 24 hours a day and that 'there is always a full team of officers in there', presumably filing paper.

It didn't do your fellow councillor much good when she found herself unable to get a response from Macclesfield Police Station in the middle of the day when boots and fists were flying just outside the station. I don't suppose that for one minute she stopped to think, 'Never mind that I am stuck outside in the middle of this riot, at least I am witnessing the efficiency of a Divisional Central Control Operation.' The chances are that she just might have preferred the 'inefficiency' of a couple of large capable bobbies to sort things out.

We all know that policing today is a tough job and all things considered our bobbies do a pretty good job. Most of us are usually pleased to see them but, like our ageing parents and grown-up children, we don't see enough of them. So *please* don't keep repeating 'Official Policy' and quoting the 'Criminal Justice Act' because terrified old ladies and young boys with broken noses won't understand. We pay politicians and senior police officers to worry about that stuff. Just get our beloved bobbies out of the stationery cupboard and onto the streets, where they were always meant to be.

Yours faithfully,

Vic Barlow

---

16 November 1999

Dear Sir,

I JUST CAN'T HELP IT

I would like to know if any readers have been beset with the affliction with which I find myself suffering, namely the involuntary urge to blurt out the word 'prat' immediately after the name 'William Hague'. Not that I am a Labour supporter. Only recently I heard that Disney are making a follow-up to 'The Lion King' starring Foreign Secretary Robin Cook entitled 'The Lying Git'.

Generally speaking most politicians want to appear Angels and the sooner the better. But how on earth are we ever going to get rid of 'Smiler' from 10 Downing Street when 'Tory Boy' is our only alternative?

However much Tony grates on your nerves can you possibly imagine sending Willy Boy off to Baghdad or Warsaw to negotiate on our behalf in his baseball cap. I suppose there's always the chance that both regimes would be crippled by laughter.

So, if William is not going to help rid us of 'He of the Satanic Grin' then Tory Boy must be replaced and I think I know just the man. I love Nick Winterton, he's been to my house, he's visited my kids' school, he's been to every village fête I've ever attended, he's christened pigs and drank with princes. He's like The Holy Ghost, He is omnipresent. That said, and credit given where credit's due, it's time he moved on.

He's been on our shelves a long time and I think he's passed his sell-by date. So, what better move could there be than for our man Nick to replace Tory Boy as Leader and become the next Prime Minister?

John Prescott would undoubtedly get the smacking he so richly deserves. Ireland would be towed across the Atlantic to Boston and moored in a marina as a tourist attraction. Child crime would be slashed as juveniles across the country were shown pictures of Jeffrey Archer and told 'this is what will happen to you if you keep telling lies'.

And finally, the ubiquitous face of Nick would disappear at last from our local paper, to be replaced by a new Tory MP, but who? ... on no, surely no ... not him ... prat ...

Yours faithfully,

Vic Barlow

---

22 November 1999

Dear Sir,

INTO THE MILLENNIUM!

As the new millennium approaches I would like to offer you my predictions for our great town in the coming century.

2000: Following the trend set by Bill and Hilary Clinton in naming their daughter 'Chelsea', 'The Blair Tich Project' materialises with the birth of the Prime Minister's new son whom he names 'Paddington'.

2001: Sammy McIlroy becomes manager of Northern Ireland; Macclesfield bobbies join official register of Endangered Species.

2002: Nick Winterton becomes Prime Minister; Macclesfield Borough Council changes its name to 'Jones Homes'; first brick laid for Macclesfield's new Multiplex Cinema.

2003: Marks and Spencer demolished; train fare to London from Macclesfield raised to £500; after a wet Wednesday, new housing development in Bollin Valley near Beech Farm Drive submerged under water.

2004: huge new 10,000 all-seater stadium opens up to house the 900 people that now go to watch Macclesfield football Team; Victoria Park Flats re-sited on old Moss Rose football ground, sold as 'Executive Town Houses' and re-named 'The Villains'; calls to Macclesfield Police re-routed to London.

2005: plans approved to turn Macclesfield Forest into massive new housing development of 'Executive' log cabins; Marks and Spencer re-opens as Charity Shop with much improved clothing range.

2006: second brick laid in Macclesfield's new multiplex cinema; train fare to London £1000.

2007: last Macclesfield policeman bred in captivity retires.

2008: calls to Macclesfield Police re-routed via Brussels; homes in the Bollin Valley now only accessible by trawler.

2009: plans to develop Teggs Nose as Manchester Airport's third runway are approved. Developers claim that having a runway so high up will save fuel for aircraft coming down.

2010: third brick laid for new multiplex cinema.

2011: Macclesfield Police are now only available through their website, www.copout.com.

2012: Nick Winterton crowned King. Jones Homes mark the occasion by donating the last square yard of open land as a children's play area, but charge for access.

2014: Macclesfield Police introduce a new Emergency Service where an image of a Macclesfield bobby can now be digitally enhanced and downloaded to your computer at the touch of a key.

2015: train fare to London from Macclesfield now same price as a minor Brazilian soccer Player; homes in the Bollin Valley now declared suitable only for crustaceans.

Have a Great Millennium,

Vic Barlow

---

9 December 1999

Dear Sir,

ALL FOR ONE

As the Macclesfield Express frequently testifies, we have vulnerable old ladies being attacked in broad daylight, mentally ill people living rough on our freezing streets and chronically sick people dying while they wait for hospital treatment – so what has this Government chosen to worry about? Too many clubs that don't treat men and women equally!

It may be some comfort to the poor old lady who was mugged, battered and dragged off her feet to know that at least in future she'll always be able to get a game of Rugby at Macclesfield Rugby Club. And should you be some elderly desperate man awaiting urgent treatment for your prostate well, never mind, at least you'll be able to join the W. I. while you're waiting.

It would be laughable if a change of government would stop us being subjected to the ideas of politically correct morons but, as we know from our previous experience, this is a forlorn hope.

After thirty years of horrific, mind-numbing atrocities in Ulster what was the first decision taken by the new Northern Ireland Assembly? Was it never again to resort to armed conflict? Perhaps it was to make a personal apology and a plea for forgiveness from every person maimed or injured by three decades of madness? Afraid not.

The first decision they took was to increase their own salaries from twenty-nine to thirty-eight thousand pounds. It's probably the only decision they will *ever* make on which they were unanimous.

That's it from me folks. It's Christmas, Goodwill to All Men and all that.

No more moaning. I'm off to join the Young Wives.

Have a Wonderful Christmas.

Vic Barlow

---

15 January 2000

Dear Sir,

PET SHOP BOYS

May I say through your august columns how flattered I was to read Councillor Flynn's most generous comments regarding my humble contribution to the Macclesfield Express. My flabber was further gasted when I saw that my 'Millennium Letter' was printed in two successive editions. What an accolade. What recognition. So good they named it twice!

This state of Celebrity sadly came to an abrupt end at the check-out in Pet Smart when a young lad asked on seeing my Credit Card

"You Vic Barlow that writes them letters?"

I confirmed my identity and asked him if he was a regular reader.

"No but my dad is and he thinks you're a prat."

All of which brings me to my somewhat cynical personality and how it came to be. In the late sixties I was a young man trying to make a living as a stand-up Comedian. I toured the pubs and clubs of the North-West dying painfully night after night until one dark wet evening at a Working Men's Club on the Wirral. I had spent an agonising half-hour on stage telling joke after joke to ... complete and total silence!

In an effort to end this unmitigated torture I blurted out my final story. Then, to my utter astonishment, a lone person began to clap in the darkness.

"Thank you, thank you so much for that applause," I cried, truly grateful. To which came the reply in a thick Scouse accent "I wasn't applauding pal. I was just getting the sauce out of the bottle."

Some months later I phoned a Concert Secretary in Yorkshire for whom I had agreed to do a Sunday Lunchtime Talent Contest the previous week and inquired why no bookings had come my way as a result.

"Well lad," he began "some acts dunna get bookings coz them's too expensive, and some dunna get bookings coz them's too fussy, but the reason tha's got no bookings is coz tha's crap."

Thus ended a promising Show Biz. career.

So, I do hope that Mr Flynn and the good people of the Macclesfield Express will forgive me if I appear ungrateful to 'Visitors Offering Praise' – it's just that it always seems to get neutralised by Concert Secretaries and Pet Shop Boys bearing Truth.

Yours faithfully,

Vic Barlow

---

30 January 2000

Dear Sir,

YOUR MONEY OR YOUR LIFE

An opening paragraph from last week's Macclesfield Express began "Planing councillors failed to persuade colleagues to turn down £50,000 from the Beech Lane developers". No Kidding! Statistically there is more chance of being attacked by a platypus!

Anyone who watches "Who Wants to be a Millionaire?" will be aware that contestants have to answer 15 questions before they make a million. In Macclesfield, developers don't have to answer *any* questions to acquire the same amount (although they may need to 'phone a friend').

Whatever the justification for the payment of such a large amount, one cannot help but be reminded of that famous lesson in morality posed by Sir Winston Churchill. When he asked a female critic if she would consider sleeping with a man she had only just met for a million pounds, she gave an unequivocal "Yes!"

When asked again if she would do the same for five pounds, the outraged woman exploded. "What do you think I am – a prostitute?" – to which Winston replied, "We've already established what you are, we are just negotiating the price."

Finally, I would like to say how affronted I feel to see developers trooping freely in and out of our Town Hall without any attempt at disguise. Even Dick Turpin had the decency to wear a mask.

Yours faithfully,

Vic Barlow

3 February 2000

Dear Sir,

DID HE OR DIDN'T HE?

Having just read the story in today's Macclesfield Express regarding PC Austin Reid (Feb 2nd) can I appeal for someone to help me out on this saga? We have a local beat bobby with an exemplary record who allegedly asks a 20-year-old black man in Prestbury what he's doing and if he has a 'criminal record'? A question apparently so intimidating that the man involved says he "doubts whether he will ever recover".

OK, no one got killed, hurt or even arrested but given the delicate state of the police reputation towards ethnic minorities I can understand the Cheshire Police Complaints Authority wanting to check this out.

Did PC Reid actually say what was alleged and, if so, was it really offensive? How long do we, the uneducated public, think it should take to arrive at an answer to this simple question? All day? A couple of days? A week?

Apparently not. After ten months of 'ongoing investigations' Cheshire Police say they are still investigating because "It's more important to get it right than get it done quickly".

Ten Months! The gestation period for an elephant is not much longer than this.

Aren't we lucky The Great Train Robbery didn't occur in Cheshire! We'd have all been dead before we found out who done it. I don't wish to be insensitive to the young man involved but there is also a well-respected local bobby here living under a nasty cloud and a local community desperate for good, experienced policemen.

So please can we see some action from the Top Brass? It's not that difficult.

You can 'Phone a Friend' or even go Fifty-Fifty – but for goodness sake, make a decision.

Yours faithfully,

Vic Barlow

---

15 February 2000

Dear Sir,

FAMINE IN THE HILLS!

I write to you from a dark, isolated leaf-strewn 'B' Road somewhere in Derbyshire. Despite several days of exhausting travel I have to report that as yet I have had no success in getting through to the beleaguered village of Rainow.

I started my travels last Sunday from Sutton. A simple enough journey down to the Tesco Roundabout, right up Hurdsfield Road and then ... a total blockade. Road closed, sand-bagged, barricaded, dug up; in a 'No-One Shall Pass' kind of way (though strangely, not affecting the entrance to the mighty Tesco). This was definitely a No-Go Area.

Never one to give in easily I decided to drive on to Adlington and enter Rainow via Pott Shrigley ... until ... I met a sign at the end of the Silk Road stating 'Road Works for 25 weeks.'

Jeremy Clarkson and A. A. Gill were also stuck in the traffic trying to get to Rainow, so I redirected them towards Prestbury (nice guys!)

By now I had abandoned the car, rented a Llama and decided to trek up Buxton Road and down Bull Hill only to find that it too was closed.

Exactly what is going on? While Macclesfield councillors dither and blather on about their 'statutory obligations under The Highways Act' people in Rainow are dying. Starving to death one by one in their mountain village, cut off from supplies of even their most basic needs like Lottery Tickets and kebabs.

I have heard unconfirmed reports of cannibalism from a passing cyclist who lost an arm in the village while indicating right. So, before these reports become a reality, can we please have some relief? Maybe British Aerospace could organise an airlift or drop off food parcels on low flying sorties, but something must be done and done quick if the people of Rainow are ever going to make it through the winter. Christmas parcels, old clothes, and blankets should be delivered to Macclesfield Town Hall and addressed to 'The Rainow Relief Project' (A Cut-Off Community).

Yours faithfully,

Vic Barlow

---

19 February 2000

Dear Sir,

CAN YOU GUESS WHAT IT IS YET?

As an owner of several Labradors, Retrievers, cats, rabbits etc. I read with more than a passing interest your story regarding the use of Beagles for drugs testing at AstraZeneca. Before we all become completely outraged over this issue, I think it would be wise to consider the alternative. AstraZeneca is a profit-driven business, not a zoo and as such would be extremely unlikely to build specialist facilities and run a breeding programme unless the data provided was meaningful. If we all kick up enough headline-grabbing hysteria it's quite possible companies such as this would be forced to carry out their drug testing on less suitable subjects. This sounds fine until the day you discover that your angina tablets have made you irreversibly impotent. It would be little solace to then have AstraZeneca say "But we noted no adverse reaction in the comprehensive tests we carried out on pomegranates." I, for one, do not want to go to hospital with a huge unidentified growth and have Rolf Harris appear asking the Doctor, "Can you guess what it is yet?"

Obviously any humane society wants to be reassured that animals are not suffering needlessly, but this is the real world, it's not Disneyland. There are no talking pigs and singing sheep. People, real people, are suffering from cruel, crippling diseases that destroy their lives and whatever we can do to ease their suffering is a price we must be prepared to pay. There are, however, a couple of suggestions I would like to make that AstraZeneca may want to consider.

1. In view of the sensitivity of the whole Animal Testing subject it may be wise to consider carrying out this work in an unpopulated, remote location far away from the public gaze, e.g. The Millennium Dome.

2. Can I suggest also that the testing may be carried out not on dogs but on politicians, which should produce results that are more accurate and have the added benefit of causing little or no public reaction. In fact, far from public outrage, I think there may be a degree of euphoria that for once politicians

have produced something useful and as they breed like rabbits anyway the underlying costs should be minimal.

Yours faithfully,

Vic Barlow

The following letter was dictated by Max, our Golden Retriever and written down by me:

26 February 2000

Sir,

DISCIPLINE YOUR MAN!

As a Golden Retriever, Dignitary of the Clwyd Retriever Association and Fellow of the Macclesfield Forest and Canal Man Walking Society I write to express the depth of my disappointment in my fellow canines.

I have been walking my Man for some considerable time around the Borough and it is becoming increasingly difficult to find an area not totally covered with dog droppings. What are modern-day dogs coming to if they cannot even train their handlers to collect dog litter. Damned layabouts and ruffians the lot of them. A spell in the Army is what they need.

It was all very different in my day. Had I allowed my Man to ignore my litter my father would have whipped me alive. Bah! these dogs don't know they're born. I blame it on their parents – mind you, some of these so-called mongrels haven't got parents, hanging about street corners drinking puddles. No pedigree, the lot of them.

Dog Litter is exactly the same as Man Litter. It smells appalling, is incredibly infectious and spoils a damned good walk. I know puppies, dogs of good breeding, who have contracted the most horrible diseases as a result of sniffing other dog's waste.

I used to walk my Man on the canal towpath. Not any more! The place is festooned with the stuff. I then took him to Teggs Nose – same damned thing! When will these dogs ever learn that you must instil discipline into your handler or we will all pay the price.

Following this daily routine my father handed down to me would improve the environment considerably and make a Man of your handler rather than a Menace.

05.00 Hours: Reveille

05.30 Drag Man outdoors (on all-fours if need be)

05.35 Inspect Kit (Lead, 1; Whistle, 1; Pooper-scooper, 1; Bag, 1)

06.45 Walk Man to heel with short, sharp training intervals (Scoop and Bag, Scoop and Bag)

07.00 Back Home for Full Breakfast and Snooze. Repeat in early evening.

Never did me any harm and helped make me the magnificent Retriever that stands before you today.

I am Sir, your affectionate Servant, Brigadier General Sir Maxwell Tislaw (Retired)

... and Vic Barlow

15 March 2000

Dear Sir,

LOOK AT THE SIZE OF HIS DIGGER!

Is this or is this not an amazing town in which to live?

Question: What is our town's most diminishing resource?

Answer: Land

So, for what purpose do we propose to use what little land we have left ?

It would surely have to be something desperately needed by all the Community to justify its use. Wrong! The plan is for more unnecessary retail sites and a controversial football stadium that no-one is sure will ever be fully utilised. Madness, you may be forgiven for thinking.

Ah, but it gets better, not only does our council not agree on who actually owns the current site but have actively encouraged the developers not to illustrate a football stadium on their proposals at all. Then, from four competing developers they have chosen one but insist that it is *not* his proposal that will be built. Apparently, he was chosen on the size of his JCB's.

So, to recap. We have a dwindling, finite amount of land in our town. We propose to build something of which we are not quite sure but probably is a state-of-the-art soccer stadium, together with additional retailers we don't need, on land we are not sure who owns, by a developer whose plans we have not adopted.

Now, one might be forgiven for thinking that with all the housing development that has taken place around Macclesfield in the past decade, a serious plan for children's neighbourhood playing fields might have crept into town planning somewhere along the line – but apparently not. Modern kids obviously do not need to play outside in open fields any more. What they long for is a new Asda!

Surely there are more than enough 'brown sites' around the centre of town to satisfy the needs of those Retailers clamouring at our gates and no doubt we can learn to struggle by without another expensive, posey leisure centre. The current footie ground is not beyond being remodelled, given the dedication of fans and directors – so why not leave what little we have left of our open spaces … open? The proposal for a Multiplex cinema, wanted by far more Maxonians than this proposed development was duly refused – so why rush ahead with this one?

Could it possibly be that open fields for kids to play on make money for no one? Are we being driven by an insatiable commercial force that will never rest until every conceivable open space around Macclesfield is covered with concrete?

Yours faithfully,

Vic Barlow

25 March 2000

Dear Sir,

UPWARDLY MOBILE!

Hee ... Hee...Hee.. Oh no ... Hee... Heeeee! Please forgive me but I'm sat on the London train reading today's Macclesfield Express with a hankie stuffed in my mouth to suppress my hysterics. Hold on a minute ... I'll just dry my eyes. Right, that's better, now where were we? Oh yes – the rejection of the plan for an Orange mobile phone mast. This is a beautiful story and I urge any-one who has not bought a Macclesfield Express dated March 22nd to obtain one without delay.

The Council, God bless'em, has decided in its supreme wisdom that they do not intend to permit the siting of a mobile phone mast at the top of Park Lane because, according to Coun. Stephen Carter, "Young people have these phones and are using them when their heads and minds are still growing". Oh, Stephen, if only the same thing could be said for our councillors.

He then goes on to say that mobile phones "could be the next BSE." On this point I do share his concern and urge all farmers here and now not to allow their cattle to make any more than one off-peak phone call per cow, per day.

Another reason for the Council's rejection was that although designed to look like a lamp-post the mast would be "visually intrusive". Are you kidding? How about a rash of cast iron 'Traffic Calming' bollards shipped straight from The Falls Road to Ivy Road? Or maybe a thousand gigantic fluorescent road signs thrown onto picturesque Buxton Road, turning it into The Isle of Man TT?

Obviously, Orange made a serious error in the design of this mast. Had they stuck it at a major junction and surrounded it by a traffic island, leading to a new supermarket or placed it on the roof of another theme pub, everything would have been hunky-dory. But disguised as a simple lamp-post, it was al-ways a non-starter.

If Orange aspire to be a major player in mobile communications they have to do better than this. Remember – this is Macclesfield. Show some imagination. Think big! Wrap your mast around a football stadium fit to host the next World Cup or, better still, slap it in the middle of the Green Belt and say those magic words 'Executive Homes' and – no problemo! You're in!

Simple ideas. Simple Solutions all the time! Better go now. Freda's on the mobile and I daren't ignore her. She's a real cow.

Yours faithfully,

Vic Barlow

---

31 March 2000

Dear Sir,

TELL IT LIKE IT IS!

As everyone knows I love Macclesfield and I am extremely proud of our football club and its supporters, therefore I'd like to save them from the uncertainty and confusion surrounding the development plans for a new stadium.

I have talked to a lot of councillors who have clarified for me the exact situation. When the Committee met to choose a developer, some of them didn't agree with the choice made. Some of them thought that we shouldn't be developing anything; others thought we should, but weren't sure what. Those that thought we should duly chose a developer. Those that thought we should not left in disgust, which only left those that *thought* we should. But they weren't sure of what!

The 'ones that thought we should' didn't know that 'the ones that weren't sure what' had told all the competing developers not to show a football stadium on their plans. So 'the ones that thought we should' didn't know what 'the ones that weren't sure what' knew and 'the ones that thought we should not' had left too early to know what 'the ones that weren't sure what' had done.

Now some of 'the ones that said we should not' said they weren't sure who owned the land anyway. So, in theory, 'the ones that said we should' could be developing something – we're not sure what – on land we're not sure where.

When 'the ones that said we should but weren't sure what' do know what, they're going to tell 'the ones that said we should' and 'the ones who said we should not'. Then 'the ones that said we should not' before they actually knew what might finally agree with 'the ones that said we should' and 'the ones that said we should but weren't sure what' now that everyone knows what's what.

You can't have it simpler than that!

Yours faithfully,

Vic Barlow

3 April 2000

Dear Sir,

DOGGIE DOINGS DOWN WHIRLEY WAY

I sympathise totally with those mums in Whirley Road regarding their dog-poop problems. I have had a German Shepherd defecating on my front lawn every morning for months. Scolding and chasing him off has proved useless. The problem has gone from bad to worse and I noticed recently that his dog is now doing it as well!

A friend of mine decided to shame the owners of dogs that used his open-plan front garden as a toilet by placing little flags with the name of the dog's owner on the deposits. Unfortunately he then went away on holiday and came back to find that a local rugby team passing by on their way home from the pub thought it was some kind of competition and decided to leave their own individual contributions. (A hooker by the name of Harvey was judged to have won!)

Perhaps some national coverage on Crimewatch UK might help.

"Good evening this is Nick Ross and tonight police in Macclesfield (obviously this is fictitious as there are no police in Macclesfield) are looking for the culprits who left these deposits on Whirley Road" (pan to said deposits) "Witnesses say that one perpetrator was a black male, with brown pointed ears and penetrating eyes and the other was a middle-aged female with a long nose and extremely hairy legs. Several additional deposits have appeared today which police are delving into."

My advice to the people of Whirley Road is 'be vigilant' – this is an odious crime that needs careful handling or it could explode in your face. Please don't have nightmares!

Yours faithfully,

Vic Barlow

---

11 April 2000

Dear Sir,

A LOAD OF BULL!

I was recently scanning some old copies of the Macclesfield Express and I thought you would like to hear about an article I found regarding a Mr Frank Evans dated Jan12, 1967. Mr Evans was, wait for it, an English Bullfighter training in Spain but working part time as a Sales Rep for F. Dunkley in Hulley Road, Macclesfield.

There is a magnificent picture of him decked out in his matador outfit. He explains away his dual employment by saying that, at the Spanish ranch where he trains, they 'only fight bulls in the morning so, to "stop you getting bored", you need something to do in the afternoon'. Isn't that a beautiful quote?

The Macclesfield Express reporter does not disappoint either as he goes on to say that "So far, Mr Evans has not been seriously gored, so he is going to continue to fight bulls for another five years and, if nothing has happened by then, he's coming home."

It's reassuring to know that, even in 1967, there were as many amazingly eccentric people in Macclesfield as there are today and that the reporting in The Macclesfield Express was as wonderfully wacky then as it is now!

Kind regards,

Vic Barlow

8 April 2000

Dear Sir,

HISTORIC NOTICE

In view of the plethora of notices posted on Byrons Lane regarding forthcoming road works could I possibly, through the generosity of your pages, issue the following notice:

ON BEHALF OF THE RESIDENTS OF SUTTON & LANGLEY

To All Persons Be They Resident, Vagrant, Miscreant, Vagabond, Officer of The Crown, Engineer, Labourers, Purveyors of Cable or Pipe or any other Ne'er-do-wells.

Would the aforesaid persons desirous of damaging, digging, blocking, excavating, causing explosion to, flooding of, burning down or any other such activity hindrous to the free flow of non-horse-drawn transportation along Byrons Lane please gather together as one with their implements at dawn on April12th in the year of our Lord 2000. There to go about their business with such force and abandonment, that thereafter Byrons Lane be left free of interference in perpetuity.

Any Tradesman, Navvy or Surveyor found to be on site or returning to Byrons Lane with intent to dig beyond the end of the month of April shall be held in the stocks within Prestbury Village until the end of this millennium or until such time as a Multiplex Cinema be constructed in Macclesfield town, whichever shall be the first occurrence.

Yours faithfully,

Vic Barlow

---

27 April 2000

Dear Sir,

FIND A FRIEND

So Councillor Mike Flynn thinks an advert in the Macclesfield Express explaining the Moss Rose development (or lack of) would put things right, does he? What a spiffing idea and, with local elections coming up on 4th May, perhaps expanding this concept would be timely.

What I suggest is that each councillor runs an advert in the excellent Macclesfield Express 'Find A Friend' page along the lines of:

"Active Conservative Lady with huge assets and enormous majority seeks loving builder for long-term relationship beneficial to both."

"Confused, Liberally minded gentleman interested in football stadiums, leisure centres and Asda WLTM intelligent male/female with GSOH and own teeth to explain what's going on in Macclesfield."

"Brilliant, socially minded female with high profile celebrity name WLTM young dynamic Prime Minister for drooling over and idolising."

Yours faithfully,

Vic Barlow

This was my tongue-in-cheek reply to Coun Ken Thompson after he blasted me for criticising him 'without knowing all the facts.'

---

23 July 2000

Dear Sir,

I read with due deference Coun Ken Thompson's letter of chastisement for my recent 'scurrilous' comments. So, what is it you want me to do in future?

★ Do my homework

★ Listen more carefully

★ Make sure I have all the facts

★ Come to a sensible conclusion and ...

★ Act accordingly.

OK Ken – got it!

Interesting concept coming from a councillor though, don't you think?
Kind regards,

Vic Barlow

---

30 July 2000

Dear Sir,

GOD BLESS AMERICA

I recently entertained an American friend on his visit to Macclesfield and feel I should give unsuspecting Maxonians the benefit of my experience. He arrived from London by train and, after an effusive greeting, asked me why his train fare from Euston was almost as much as his air fare from New York? I explained about British Rail and Richard Branson to which he observed "So, Branson, your 'Friend of the People' takes over the train service and doubles the fares in two years. Some 'Friend'!"

I bundled him out of the station and into my car quickly so as not to be overheard and drove to the shops at Tytherington. As we travelled down Brocklehurst Avenue we narrowly missed an oncoming vehicle circumnavigating the 'traffic calming' bollards.

"Hey Vic, when your City Council find out some cowboy contractor has left cast iron buoys out in the middle of the road they are gonna be pretty mad." I decided not to enlighten him.

The following day he wanted to see a game of 'your soccer' and so I took him to Moss Rose. He remarked on the small crowd and I proudly told him that there was a plan for a new all-seater 10,000-capacity stadium. He asked me how the club could afford it with such poor attendances and I explained that a developer was offering to provide it for free.

"So, lemme get this straight Vic," he remarked later in a most annoying fashion, "You gotta soccer team that is watched by less than 2000 and a developer is gonna build you a stadium for 10,000 and do it all for free?" I was beginning to dislike Americans.

"Ain't no such thing as a Free Lunch, Vic," he rapped "Sounds to me like some Big Money people have another agenda going." At this point, I was burning with indignation and we left the ground in silence.

On his last full day he wanted to go shopping so I took him into town only to find all the car parks full with the exception of Jordangate. "This ain't no convenient 'Parking Lot' for shoppers," he commented and then on seeing the Town Hall added "But it sure is great for those guys over at City Hall." He then asked me where the other 'Parking Lots' were and I explained to him that it was where he had seen the market. "So, if your market has taken over the parking lots, what happens in your Market Square?" I ignored the question. And the next one asking where the 'Movies' were.

On the way home to Sutton we went down the Silk Road and while we crawled along Mill Lane in the heavy traffic he asked me about Leek and its importance as a destination.

Sitting back in my car he tried to summarise aloud the information I gave him. "So you build a modern highway filtering into a narrow congested lane that leads to a town no one goes to?"

Mercifully it was a brief visit and I was able to deposit him back at the station the following morning and with the words 'Have a Nice Day' ringing in my ears I waved my interrogator farewell.

Yours faithfully,

Vic Barlow

Part 3: Barlow's Brief

Following some early articles I wrote, and the publication of my letters, the Macc Express invited me to do a weekly column. Since then, I have been tormented by taxi drivers, crucified by councillors and berated by bobbies. Did I deserve it? They're all in here.

See what you think ...

---

16 February 1997

This was a little piece I wrote in response to Nick Winterton's reaction to the Macclesfield Express's support of Wizard Radio when the local Radio Franchise was being decided upon.

Radio Wars

Regardless of your political persuasion I am sure you will agree that Nick Winterton is without doubt one of the more conscientious Members of Parliament. He opens things, closes things, rails against things, proposes things. He is, it has to be said, a great doer of 'things'.

There are critically ill patients unable to find hospital beds, old-age pensioners struggling to survive on an income insufficient to feed a gerbil, and the unrelenting onslaught of the drug culture upon our precious children all clamouring for attention. One wonders how any human being, no matter how conscientious, can decide which issues to champion.

It came therefore as something of a surprise to find that, out of this plethora of human misery, the Macclesfield Express article on Wizard Radio has so incurred his wrath that it has risen to the top of his agenda. He was apparently 'appalled' at the 'gross abuse of editorial impartiality'.

He may have a point. It may have been presumptuous in its implication that Wizard would win the much-coveted Local Radio Franchise. It may also be that, as long as we have a good local radio station, free of Chris Evans, generally speaking the rest of us don't give a toss.

The point is, Nick, that whilst we all have aged friends and relatives to worry about, and our children's health and welfare over which to agonise, we are, regrettably, indifferent to the name of Radio Whatever. It is, I admit, possible that in a Christmas yet to come some homeless unfortunate languishing in a frozen Chestergate may be so incensed by hearing Wizard Radio emanating from a passing vehicle that he forgoes the succour and comfort afforded him by the doorway of Russell Kellar's excellent establishment and, adorned only in a sandwich board, disappears towards Mill

Street screaming 'Impartiality in Local Radio Licensing.' It is possible ... but probably not in our lifetime.

Priorities Nick, priorities.

---

15 December 1997

Lord Tim

In a fit of indignation I wrote a letter to the Macclesfield Express relating to the pointless ongoing prosecutions of self styled Lord Tim Hudson for failing to demolish his impressive but unapproved wrought iron gates at Birtles, a small picturesque hamlet inhabited only by the wealthiest of the Cheshire Set and, of course, Lord Tim himself.

Returning home I was somewhat taken aback by the polished voice on my answerphone inviting me down to 'Birtles Bowl' to 'hear The Tim Hudson Story'. Over the years I had caught brief sightings of Lord Tim but had never actually visited him in his natural habitat. As he is nearing his sixtieth birthday, I thought it time I went. "Come soon," the voice urged, "I have a TV crew here doing a documentary on me right now." How could I resist?

I found Birtles Lane, between Macclesfield and Chelford, turned off the road and pulled up alongside a ramshackle wooden cricket pavilion. It was a dark overcast day. Large flags flapped lazily around the creaking building and carrion crows called out from a nearby tree, I felt uncharacteristically nervous. Stepping out of the car I locked the door behind me. No Tim, no TV crew, nothing.

Suddenly, out of nowhere he was there, beside me, in my face, invading my personal space. "Hey Man do you want to know what's going on in this town. There's a conspiracy man. This is Watergate in Macclesfield."

"More Birtles Gate", I responded but the humour was lost, Lord Tim was transmitting not receiving.

"This is war man, they want to wreck me, bury me, scrape the dead flesh from my bones." I began to wonder if writing a few letters to my local paper qualified me for this assignment. "They are all in it together man, they just want to destroy my dream." I needed to find calmer water.

"Do you have any animals up here Tim?" I asked in my best 'pass the butter' voice.

"Animals? Animals? Yes, of course I have animals — a horse, a rabbit and four crows. It's a conspiracy you know — they're all in on it." If I didn't know I was certainly beginning to get the picture.

He offered to make me a cup of tea in the erstwhile cricket pavilion he now calls home but gave up when he could not work out how to light the Calor gas cooker. He showed me his monumental scrap books and photo albums of his Rock 'n' Roll years in California, articles written about his skill at the wicket for various cricket teams and most of all the building of his beloved Birtles Bowl. This was his 'Dream', to build a cricket field of such beauty that the finest players in the world would willingly play there watched by an appreciative crowd basking in the summer sunshine of his Cheshire paradise.

It is, of course the Birtles Bowl venture that has so alienated him from the local community. A penchant for psychedelic decoration, raucous rock and roll parties and a long history of rebellion are not qualities destined to endear him to the readers of *Cheshire Life*.

Later, we wandered around the grounds that have for over a decade been at the epicentre of bitter dispute. Lord Tim's American wife Maxie appeared behind an enormous hedge which, for some inexplicable reason, she was attempting to trim with a tiny pair of scissors. She made me tea (she knew how to light the cooker) and explained that both their water and electricity had been disconnected by a neighbour and that they had been forced to sell all they possessed to fight the numerous legal battles waged against them by both the community and Macclesfield Borough Council.

She showed me their 'Birtles Bowl' sign painted with loving hands that had been pelted with mud and, more frighteningly, a contractors sign on their land clearly struck by a bullet from a small calibre rifle.

The Hudsons have had money, BIG money, but it came and went with the celebrities who once graced their table at Birtles Hall (now sold). Like David Platt erstwhile captain of the England soccer team who planned to come and live next door but left never to return, or Ian Botham whose marriage, according to Botham, they almost wrecked.

It seems that relationships with the Hudsons are, at best, transient. That their behaviour has embarrassed and antagonised their wealthy neighbours is indisputable. The patience of the Macclesfield Borough Council has probably been tested to breaking point and yet none of this has been brought about by their cunning or deception; the Hudsons are incapable of either. Ask a question, you get an immediate answer – it's a reflex. It may be a misguided answer but it is genuine. Much of their money, I surmise, has been lost by such lack of guile.

"What would you really like to achieve at this stage in your life?" I asked Maxie directly. I expected the restoration of previous wealth and the damnation of all enemies to be high on the list, so I was touched when she replied simply "To live more peacefully with my neighbours and to help my husband complete his 'Dream'."

There is no doubt that despite all the hardship Lord Tim has such love for this small piece of Cheshire that he would willingly lay down his life for his 'Dream'. He has made mistakes along the way, the price has been high and now he clings on stubbornly in an old wooden hut without water or electricity and calls it 'the most beautiful place on earth'.

Sadly, had the Hudsons been gay or from some ethnic minority, political correctness would demand they be viewed more charitably, but this is not the case. In fact Lord Tim belongs to one of the few endangered species it is still legal to persecute, i.e. The Impoverished Eccentric: vilified and ridiculed for his inability or unwillingness to conform.

As the Festive Party Season approaches and friends gather to drink fine wine and exchange pleasantries, the Hudsons phone will not ring. When incandescent Christmas lights illuminate the whole of Cheshire they will not chase the shadows from the Hudsons dimly lit wooden hut. And, as complaining chauffeurs scrape snow and ice from the windscreens of waiting limousines, the Hudsons will melt it and make tea. Such is the price of a 'Dream'.

Battle lines were drawn long ago. The Influential and Wealthy on one side. The Hudsons cornered and dangerous on the other. No love lost, no corner given. But need it be so? Everything has its time, people grow old, priorities change, nothing is forever and perhaps now is *the* time for all concerned to make amends, to reach a compromise, if not to actually embrace then to accept each others idiosyncrasies and live with less conflict and more harmony. If South Africa and Ulster can do it after centuries of bloodshed surely the Hudsons and the good people of Birtles can find their own path to understanding.

I would like to think that in years to come when the ghosts of Tim and Maxie Hudson walk the fields of Birtles hand in hand, as they surely will, that they remember not the bitter, dark winters spent in isolation from resentful neighbours but that point in time when they finally came together in mutual respect and allowed each other to pursue their 'Dream'. That, indeed, would be a Christmas worthy of the name.

---

15 December 1999

The following was a response given to The Macclesfield Express who asked me how I would like to spend Millennium Eve and with whom.

New Year's Eve, 1999

I may not be able to be at any Millennium Party because we lost my dad this week. He's not dead, he's somewhere in IKEA. Given a completely open choice of whom I would like to sit next to at The Millennium Party I would definitely chose Lassie. Every New Year's Eve I always end up with a dog so I might as well pick one that I like. This would give me a golden

Me and Mrs B on New Year's Eve, 1999

opportunity to discuss something that has been puzzling me for a long, long, time: whatever happened to *white* dog poop? They used to be tons of it all over the place then one day we woke up and ... nothing ... gone ... not a dollop to be seen. I've been trying to solve this for years. It's like the X-Files, no-one knows. Perhaps Lassie will tell.

As for food, I would eat as much English Beef as I could get my hands on. How dare the French and Germans criticise our meat. Some of their women are bigger than our cows!

As far as alcohol is concerned, I don't drink as a rule. I do as a habit, but not as a rule. Therefore, I think I would have to go to Yates's for a pint of Ann Boleyn (No Head.) – it's so flat, they serve it in envelopes.)

My New Year's wish for Y2K would be that me and the wife finally make it to Texas. I've always wanted to go there, but she prefers B&Q.

---

19 April 2000

Fame At Last

OK I give in! Since the Macclesfield Express decided to do a profile of yours truly and publish an old photo of me as a child ventriloquist with a

Which one's the dummy?

grotesque dummy I feel like Salman Rushdie. If anyone else says 'brilliant picture of you and the dummy, which one's which?' I just might do something very unsavoury.

I've had smirking filling station girls asking me to sign their copy of the Macclesfield Express and pubescent schoolboys shouting 'tell us a joke Dummy' from the safety of their school bus and most bazaar of all a message on my answer phone from some odd-ball who's convinced that I'm really Jimmy Clitheroe.

The Coup de Grace was finally delivered by an elderly lady in the Covered Market who said "I saw you in the Macc Express." Beaming with recognition I nodded my newly acquired Celebrity Nod.

"Wonderful you are." I was in no hurry to run off. "Wonderful," she repeated.

This was more like it. I offered to buy her tea and she asked for a cream bun as well. Still, you can't be too generous to your fans I reasoned, settling down opposite to receive more adulation.

"My sister likes you as well," I raised my eyebrows in a Roger Moore type gesture of mock surprise.

"She loved that programme of you on the telly."

I started to feel a little uneasy, having never actually been on telly, "But I'm not sure that the Royal family approves of you following them around everywhere taking pictures. And the Queen Mother didn't seem to like you stopping her in the street."

"I think you'll find that the person you're talking about is actually Colin Edwards," I snapped tartly.

"Oh no you're wrong. It was definitely the Queen Mother."

At this point I must confess I did consider forcing her to spit out the bun and wrestling her arm up her back for the £1.20 tea money.

So, everyone's had their fun. Can we now please forget all about it and get back to business as usual.

26 April 2000

Council Rules

I have to confess that I, like 95% of Maxonians, have never actually been to a Council Meeting but from some of the reports we read from various Councillors I have a pretty good idea how they are conducted:

Con. Councillor: Fellow Members of Macclesfield Borough Council. I would like to move a motion that: 'This Council deplores measures taken in the Labour Government's recent Budget.'

Lab. Councillor: No, we don't.

Con. Councillor: Don't what?

Lab. Councillor: 'Deplore', We don't do 'deploring' any more. We stopped 'deploring' in 1997 as soon as we got a Labour Government. We do 'Fawning and Admiration' now.

Con. Councillor: This Council would further like to debate our stance on Third World Debt.

Lib Dem. Councillor: Excuse me, but there's a developer at the door wants to know if he can build something huge at Lyme Green.

Con. Councillor: Don't interrupt. We're trying to have a serious debate in here on world affairs.

Lib Dem. Councillor: Actually there's four of them out there and they all want to build something huge.

Lab. Councillor: Don't you think we need to choose *one* developer ?

Con. Councillor: Oh for God's sake! Get them to do Scissors, Paper, Stone like we usually do and we'll go with whoever wins.

Lib Dem. Councillor: OK, You're the boss.

Con. Councillor: Now can we discuss this Government's prevarication on the European Single Currency?

Lib Dem. Councillor: Excuse me.

Con. Councillor: Yes, what is it now?

Lib. Dem. Councillor: Crosby Homes want to slap up some houses in Kerridge.

Con. Councillor: Well tell them to get 'slapping' and stop interrupting. Now can we move on to events in South East Asia?

Lab. Councillor: Never mind South East Asia. What about the three-quarters of a million pounds *overpayment* of benefits our own Council paid out last year?

Con. Councillor: What about it?

Lab. Councillor: Can we talk about that?

Con. Councillor: No, it's a secret.

Lab. Councillor: Can we talk about the Council Budget for this year?

Con. Councillor: That's a secret as well.

Lab. Councillor: Council Tax rises?

Con. Councillor: Sorry, secret.

Lab. Councillor: How about Chief Officer's Expenses?

Lab. Councillor: Secret.

Lib Dem. Councillor: Excuse me.

Con. Councillor: This had better be good.

Lib Dem. Councillor: I have a question that needs an answer now.

Con. Councillor: Yes, all right then. What is it?

Lib Dem. Councillor: Does Paper beat Stone?

And that my friends is how things *really* work in Macclesfield.

---

10 May 2000

Save A Centre

It's not often that I can claim to save anyone the expenditure of £5000 but this week I can do just that. Apparently, the Planning Office intends to spend £5000 on Consultants to tell them why the town centre is dying. Well, save your cash. It's simple. Any Maxonian will tell you for nothing. Here's the recipe:

- ☞ Make parking extremely difficult for everyone except Town Hall staff.
- ☞ Ensure that those who can park have to pay.
- ☞ Make sure that the Pay & Display machines don't give change.
- ☞ Encourage every major, crowd-pulling retailer to relocate out of town and give ample free parking.
- ☞ Agree to each and every application to turn town centre retail sites into grotty pubs.
- ☞ Create a Christmas Shopping Experience so bereft of joy that it makes Leek look like Disneyland.
- ☞ Finally, give the go-ahead to some huge unspecified development on the southern edge of town that will draw the last drop of commercial blood from the centre.

There, that should do it. One dead town centre.

10 May 2000

It's a 'Love' thing

Recently I was fulfilling an after dinner speaking engagement and had just started to tell a Scottish joke when a vexed voice from another table yelled "Racist!"

I moved uncomfortably on to a story concerning female drivers and a lady guest shouted "Sexist!"

In desperation I racked my brain for something non controversial and began to tell a humorous tale about Mozart and a Smart Alec nearby yelled out "Violinist!"

The following day I was speaking on the phone to a Ms. Thompson from a travel company in London and expressed my appreciation for her efforts by saying innocently "Thanks, Love." You would have thought I'd called her a female dog. She had a Dickie Fit. "Don't you 'love' me she yelled. I was going to explain that I'm just a Macclesfield Lad but she disconnected.

I'm not against women doing anything. I was brought up in a strong female environment. My mother, grandmother and most of my aunts were women but I'm still going to go for Lennox Lewis for the Heavyweight title over Vanessa.

If my bank manager or my doctor turns out to be female I'm a happy chappie. I know they'll be good. I know they probably had to try harder to succeed. I never saw the logic in all that nonsense about different pay for doing the same job and I still don't see why we can't have more women surgeons, pilots and managing directors, but let's not be completely daft.

If you are trapped in a corner on the sixth floor of a burning building with two broken legs and a minute's supply of oxygen left who do you want to see in that firefighter's outfit smashing their way towards you through the smoke? A 17-stone rugby player from Macclesfield Town or a member of Rainow Women's Institute?

Once when I thought that my wife was having a miscarriage I panicked and called in the woman next door to check things out. OK, I could have got in touch with a brickie I know down the street but something told me to go with the lady next door, all right?

There was a job advertisement that recently had to be withdrawn from a Peterborough Job Centre because it requested applications from 'Hard Working and Honest Individuals.' It was considered by the Job Centre Manager to be 'discriminatory', presumably against 'Bone Idle and Dishonest' individuals. Have we all gone completely stark staring mad?

Oh yeah and another thing – what's with all this nonsense about not calling a 'blackboard' a 'blackboard'? What do they suggest we call white-wash? The truth is we are each of us precious individuals in our own right. We all have the right to be respected and to show respect. We each have individual talents and qualities that deserve to be recognised and rewarded for what they produce.

When the lady in the Butty Bar at Lyme Green serves me a bacon barm and asks, "Do you want anything else love?" it's not an indication that she is subliminally projecting a negative image of the entire male progeny throughout the post-Ice Age era. She's just doing her job. That's it, that's all there is to it, that's the whole deal. I don't need the support of the Politically Correct Thought Police to repair my dented self esteem. So, let's not allow the insecure and the neurotic to lay down rules for how the rest of us relate to each other.

When Mrs B and I married in 1992 we agreed to do everything together. She weeds the garden with me, she cooks dinner with me. And sometimes, when she's really mad, she wipes the floor with me. That's the way it is.

We also agreed that we would never to go to bed angry. I've been awake now for over seven years!

Women don't have to hold down three jobs and do Open University to show us how smart they are, we already know. Statistics prove that most men only ever use one third of their brain anyway ... God knows what they do with the other third! Ladies, we are all in this 'Life' thing together, for better for worse. It's a team effort. An equal partnership. You don't need to ask for a vasectomy to prove it!

17 May 2000

Give Me a Break!

It was only a twelve-day holiday. That's all I took, just twelve short days and what do I return to?

Total Macclesfield chaos! I should have known. I should never have gone. I write my Macclesfield Express article before I go so as not to be late. I say nice things about people. I leave everything straight and tidy and what do I find when I come home?

Councillor Brendan Murphy bringing hell fire and damnation upon himself by insulting the gay and lesbian community in Macclesfield, and for what purpose? Personally, I always rather fancied being a Lesbian.

Not only that but he seems dead against the plan to bring ten Asylum Seekers and their families into the community. Why? We're a pretty tolerant town. Give them a chance. Let's see what their fish and chips taste like before we start criticising. And what about Councillor Peter Burns who says that there are now so many horses in the Borough that he would like to give them the vote. We've already got a Town Hall full of donkeys, so

why not? Then there's a postman apparently determined to walk back-
wards for 900 miles. I just hope our house is not on his round.

I see Cheshire Constabulary finally concluded their twelve-month
enquiry and decided to put Prestbury bobby Austin Reed back on the beat
where he belongs, proclaiming him to be a good egg after all. Nothing to do
with the public outcry at their lily-livered inability to make a decision, you
understand.

And while we are on the subject, Cheshire police are to issue a booklet
entitled 'Stop and Search' explaining how they operate. I would have
thought that 'Hide and Seek' might be more appropriate.

The Mayoress has retired, declaring that 'The Chair' is an inanimate
object and not a person. Well, it's good to know that her time in office hasn't
been wasted.

We've had a major fire, a crime spree, more complaints about dog poo,
a highway robbery and a Local Election and I only went away for twelve
days! Maybe next time I'll take the whole of Macclesfield with me then at
least I'll know what you are up to.

To be fair, the May 17th edition of the Macclesfield Express carried not
one single photograph of Nick Winterton, so it wasn't all bad news.

---

17 May 2000

It's A Cop-Out

Not too long ago, we had the frightening story of the Macclesfield councillor who found herself in the middle of a pitch battle between rival gangs of
thugs right outside the police station at midday on a Saturday. When she
broke away and ran terrified to the front door there was no-one on duty.

Now we have some poor unfortunate lady who has been attacked by a
couple of muggers yards from the Police Station in Brunswick Street.
Police say it was probably because it's a 'very secluded part of town'.

Well of course it's secluded. That's the whole point of all the letters and
representations made continually by residents. The whole of Macclesfield
is 'secluded' as far as police presence goes. It's no good some Senior Pen
Pusher in Chester giving us more waffle about how they are employing the
efficiency of a 'Central Policing Initiative' and reciting 'Official Policy' over
and over again like a Trappist Monk.

Save us the recital and get some bobbies back on the streets. We'll
make it easy, you can start with Brunswick Street and work your way out.
You'll probably find that when bobbies get used to being allowed outside
they'll quite enjoy it, once they get adjusted to seeing daylight.

24 May 2000

Mid-Life Crisis!

Isn't life cruel? I happened to be in the library last week, looking through some back issues of the Macclesfield Express, when I spotted the photograph of a most attractive lady who was a hot contender for Silk Queen 1975. I looked at her name. No, surely not, it couldn't be, but it was. It was a lady I knew. I see her in town quite often, greying hair, matronly figure, big hips, slight double chin. I was shocked. I checked the name again, it was definitely her. Good grief! What had happened to turn this lithe, latter-day lovely into Betty Turpin in just 25 short years? Surely God couldn't be so cruel as to give someone such a beautiful face and then hit it with a frying pan.

I discussed it later that night with Mrs B. who ridiculously pointed out that maybe I no longer looked as good as I had done in 1975. I excused her ignorance, undoubtedly due to the fact that I was unknown to her 25 years ago. In actual fact I still look great, hardly any change at all and to prove the point I got out one of my old photos from the seventies.

First, she pointed out that the Vic Barlow in the picture had no grey hair. In fact he had a mass of black permed curls. Not only that but she kindly indicated that the trousers worn in the photo looked decidedly smaller around the waist than the Cyrils I was currently wearing. I considered a fight but learned long ago that arguing with your wife is like trying to go through a set of revolving doors on skis.

This was a serious blow to my morale. I had always thought I looked amazingly like Tom Cruise whereas I now appeared to be a doppelgänger for John Prescott. That did it. An image update was called for and I bought myself a rowing machine on the Internet which sadly, on arrival, proved to have no oars. Never one to be easily deterred from healthy exercise I sat in it every night for a couple of weeks and just let it drift.

I then headed for one of those trendy men's fashion boutiques in Manchester and asked their advice on who was currently 'cool'. I was informed that Liam Gallagher of Oasis was just about as cool as you could get without reverting to cryogenics, which they obviously considered a serious option in my case.

I bought the obligatory Parka and a pair of very cool shades which, together with my newly acquired Gallagher swagger, made me feel I was really making progress. I wandered around Manchester city centre all day practising being Liam. I was, as they say, 'Mad for It'. Unfortunately, so was the Greater Manchester policeman who stopped me on the A6 later that evening. I was alone in my car when he asked the obligatory "Are you the driver of this vehicle sir?"

I thought of what Liam might say in these circumstances and quipped

"No pal, it's automatic — I just like sitting in the front", which I think you will agree was pretty damned 'cool'. The constable gritted his teeth and continued "Can I ask you where you were between six and seven?"

"At primary school mate," I sneered. This was great, I was really getting the hang of it now.

"Only at that time a sad middle-aged gent acting like Liam Gallagher and driving this exact vehicle left his wallet at the drive-through McDonalds in Ardwick." The game was up. The Parka went to Oxfam and the shades were 'accidentally' sat on by Mrs B. Shortly afterwards, I met my 1975 Silk Queen Contestant in Chestergate and do you know something? I thought she looked great!

---

1 June 2000

It's For Life

There have been several articles recently in the Macclesfield Express calling into question the commitment of a small number of Maxonians to their pets in general and dogs in particular. Heaven only knows how many times residents have to write to the press expressing their disgust and revulsion at the amount of dog dirt left lying all over the place by idle owners. The manager of the town's largest pet store is prosecuted for leaving three dogs starving in squalor and the Manchester Dogs' Home writes in to ask "What is wrong with the people of Macclesfield?" Apparently they have admitted 22 stray dogs from the Macclesfield area in twelve weeks and not one of them has been claimed!

That in itself has to be some sort of record for neglect. One of them is a Neapolitan Mastiff. This guy is the size of a Wildebeest. How the hell can you lose one of them and not know it? Like most people who own and care for numerous animals on a daily basis I don't get over sentimental about them, but some of the things I see and hear annoy me more than Macclesfield Council which, as most of you know, is considerable.

I stopped exercising my dogs on the canal towpath because of the solid wall of excrement left behind by irresponsible dog owners. How difficult can it be to take a polythene pooper bag with you when you go out dog walking? I have actually seen owners bring their dog to the canal in the car for the express purpose of letting it out to defecate on the tow path. Is that indolent or what?

Dogs hate to relieve themselves in their own kennel and will do almost anything to keep their personal space clean. They are not stupid — they don't want to wallow in excrement? Wouldn't you think that their owners might learn something from them, or does the dog have to spell it out? CLEAN UP!

When it comes to animal welfare, I'm afraid Disney has a lot to answer for. Goodness only knows how many Dalmatians were bred and sold after the release of his recent film but you can bet your life it was a lot more than 101. Within 12 months the 'Pets for Sale' columns in the papers were full of unwanted Dalmatians.

After the screening of the film 'Babe' hundreds of pigs were bought by private individuals as 'pets' only to be discarded when the owners found that they behaved like er ... er ... pigs.

Why do people do this? Strange as it may seem, swine can't talk, dogs don't actually dance or sing and contrary to popular myth they are not automatically your 'best friend'.

Dogs are 'fight or flight' animals which means when they encounter circumstances they dislike they either fight or, more often, run away (flight) – and that, my friends, is why so many Macclesfield dogs end up in the Manchester Dogs' home. Granted, some are simply dumped by indifferent owners but the rest have decided that their owners are, how can I put it ... 'a waste of space' and far from being their 'best friend' they have elected to 'go it alone' and take their chances. Given the total lack of any interest in their subsequent welfare you can see their point.

I see owners frequently walk their dogs off-lead along busy roads where any unexpected occurrence could put lives of dogs and drivers at risk.

No matter how much we like to credit them with human traits (God help 'em) dogs are not people. They don't need to be cosseted and indulged, but they do need to be respected. They appreciate leadership, shelter, food, and concern for their welfare – qualities which appear to be severely lacking in some Macclesfield owners.

However, to balance the record and for the sake of our reputation I would like to point out that in our Borough, we have Mr and Mrs Dudley – breeders of the 1999 International Retriever Champion (which is the highest 'Working Retriever' award in Europe). There's also Colin Pickford, one of the most prolific winners of Sheep Dog Trials in the country and Selwyn Demmy, the famous millionaire ex-bookmaker who has turned his Wilmslow home into a luxury animal shelter. All of which is somewhat reassuring, given our depressing record of ignorance and neglect.

1 June 2000

The Thinner Blue Line

Macclesfield Police are getting mighty fed-up with yours truly and as a result invited me 'down to the station' to meet Inspector Mark Whittaker who wanted to give their side of things and perhaps persuade me to tone things down a little. Well, never one to deny anyone the right to reply, I went along confidently expecting to meet an officer, with a chip on both shoulders, brimming with self importance and ready to recite Official Policy at me as though my head buttoned up the back.

I could not have been more wrong. Inspector Whittaker's been around a bit, he knows the ropes, he's a People Person. He'd give anyone a helping hand, but he's no mug. You'd like him as a neighbour and, if your son or daughter had just joined the police force, you would rest easy knowing he was the man in charge.

He's what most of us would regard as a 'proper policeman', a 'good copper' and that's just the point isn't it? We need more of his ilk. We need them on our streets now, before crimes happen, not turning up late for the inquest. He says that 'the police are doing their best with the resources available' and feels that my constant carping is 'unhelpful'.

Well I'm truly sorry about that but that's the way life is. When you are unhappy with interest rates at Barclays you don't go to the Bank of England. You complain to your local branch, the people who are accessible. They represent the Institution and it's up to them to pass the pressure on up the line.

I asked him about the number of officers employed in Macclesfield 10 years ago. He couldn't say.

I asked him about the number of officers employed in Macclesfield today. He wouldn't say.

I asked why the Austin Reed investigation took so long. 'Nothing to do with us Sir. Due entirely to the Police Complaints Authority.'

I asked about the vast amounts of police budget spent on 'early retirement'. He says it's not done in Macclesfield. Everyone's fit and healthy.

I asked about the famous unattended Front Desk. He says that when things get very busy and more officers are needed out on the street they have to leave the desk unattended. (Never works that way on the till at Tesco.)

I said that most people thought that there was far more chance of being prosecuted if you were a regular law abiding householder than if you were an habitual criminal of 'no fixed abode' with a fast car and no papers. He agreed.

I asked about not being able to call Macclesfield Police direct. And all my worst fears were confirmed.

...I LOVE THAT BIT WHERE HE GETS MUGGED!

He says that it is Official Policy that the Police Telephone Service 'move towards' Call Centres!

Well we all know what those are like, don't we?

So, don't blame Inspector Whittaker if after pressing the star key once and button one twice, followed by button three four times you have a twenty-minute wait and an earful of Greensleeves before you are informed that 'All our Agents are busy'.

Despite the efforts of Officers like Inspector Whittaker, it would appear that under the present system this is the best police service we're going to get. Forget about more policemen. It's not going to happen. Tax Inspectors ... Yes. Police inspectors ... I think not.

However what has become apparent is how suddenly Nick Winterton, along with the entire Conservative Leadership, has developed some absolutely wonderful ideas on what needs to be done to fight crime.

Unfortunately when they were actually in Government for 19 years they were totally clueless but then the Labour Party had loads of inspiration.

Now Labour are in power and they can't initiate a good idea between them.

Which just goes to illustrate what I've thought for some time, namely that we should change the System and let the Opposition of the day make Policy.

They are obviously so much better at it than any Government. They are desperate to please and totally unaffected by that 'We've got a huge majority so up yours' syndrome that seems to sap any serious intentions previously held to get the job done.

The Opposition are like eager young puppies prepared to do whatever we want, whatever is necessary so long as we learn to love them.

Personally I have always thought five years in office to be far too long for any Party. Politicians, like nappies, should be changed regularly and for the same reason.

---

7 June 2000

Just The Bare Essentials

So, what did you all make of Channel Five's Panel Game in which Keith Chegwin, together with all the contestants, appeared totally naked? I couldn't help thinking 'What a brilliant idea for a Council Meeting.' This could save our old publicity-seeking Conservative pal Coun. Brendan Murphy a shed load of time. Instead of burning the midnight oil trying to work out who to insult next in order to get into the newspapers, all he would need to do would be flash his credentials at Janet Jackson and shout "What about that for a Huge Majority?" This would definitely gain him some exposure, but from what I hear, not too many column inches. Despite his best efforts, Margaret Duddy already has her hands firmly on a Huge Majority and it's not his.

Mike Flynn of Lib. Dem. fame will undoubtedly take advantage of his party colour by arranging to have all his members coated with Fake Tan in the hope that everything comes up orange.

I think also it would be an excellent idea if developers wishing to hack up another piece of Macclesfield had to appear in the nude when they made their presentations. I wonder how eager they would be then to dump concrete on every remaining bit of grass?

It's hard to make a serious presentation for a massive new edge-of-town Retail Park when, all around, councillors are staring at you and sending out for a walnut whip. All those members of staff in the Planning Office that are currently off ill with 'stress' could come back to work and enter into the spirit of things buck naked.

You can just imagine planning chief Peter Yates commenting, "I have been looking at this proposed plan and I don't think we should recommend approval of a tunnel under the Silk Road, do you Miss Moneypenny?"

"Oh sorry Mr Yates it's not a tunnel. I've just been sitting on it."

What about the Labour councillors, The Macclesfield Six as we affectionately know them? Coun. Steven Carter, for one, is just dying to show us what he can do and, if he pops up again and it's six to four on that he will, large things are anticipated.

---

7 June 2000

Summer Fête Madness

Wasn't that a wonderful story? Every competitor in last week's Wincle Fell Race received a Trout. Yes, that's right — a trout. Not a voucher for a Domino's Pizza or a free keg of beer ... a trout!

It's just another brilliant example of Macclesfield Madness which although evident throughout the year surfaces with a vengeance in the Summer Fête Season.

Where else on God's Earth would someone dream up the idea of handing out a trout as an incentive to join in an activity almost guaranteed to send you to a cardio-vascular intensive care bed?

Let's face it, it's not the sort of purse that's going to entice the Kenyan Cross-Country Team, so who's going to volunteer for this lung bursting event on the promise of a freshwater fish?

Lunchtime drinkers from the local pub full of Dutch Courage, out of shape dads whose kids egg them on and trendy old geezers with nubile young wives who want to impress, that's who.

In a previous fête I was talked into playing a 'Fun' game of football against the Young Wives Team and was slide-tackled so savagely by a young mother that I ended up in hospital with 15 stitches in my shin. At another venue, I was press-ganged onto a tug-of-war team that was dragged half-way to White Nancy.

So, when you go to your local fête this summer, heed well the words of my old doctor who always used to say "Your body is a wonderful thing ... if you look after it it'll last you a lifetime."

14 June 2000

I Had A Dream!

I was playing Trivial Pursuit one night in a bar in Ireland when I had to ask the opposing team to name the most dangerous race in the world. (The answer was, of course, The Grand National) A glint of 'this is an easy one' passed between them before they shouted out their answer in unison which to my utter astonishment was 'Arabs'.

Fortunately I have never been prone to this kind of instant prejudice. I was brought up in a tiny post-War semi by hard-working parents who were too busy making ends meet to criticise others regardless of their persuasion.

I'm not sure my mother and father noticed anyone's colour, creed, or religion, if so they never said. My father's only concession to intolerance was that he often said he would like to find out where the Jehovah's Witnesses lived so he could go round and knock on their door when they were having their tea.

Personally, I rather like the tapestry of a multicultural society. I have my own beliefs as do many other ordinary people and just like them I keep them to myself. So why, oh why, do True Believers, people who have 'Seen The Light', insist on belting it out to anyone who will listen and even more that don't want to?

Anyone living within five miles radius of Moss Rose last Saturday evening will have had their barbecues and al fresco dinner parties regaled with the cries of Happy-Clappy People gathered together in the football ground to announce to the World how much they Truly Believed.

There's nothing wrong with being a True Believer. I admire their certainty, but why do they have to transmit it through a billion megawatt speakers on an otherwise quiet and pleasant Saturday evening? And why terminate it with an impromptu fireworks display of such earth-shattering ferocity that my dogs were convinced the end of the world was 'right nigh' and went berserk?

Anyone whose wife has been away on business for almost a week and who has planned an intimate little evening for two and has subsequently been forced to share his marital bed with four frantic, terrified Labradors is not one likely to be an easy convert.

So forgive my intolerance if I say that I'm rather hoping that the next religious rally to be held at the Moss Rose is a recruitment drive for Trappist Monks.

14 June 2000

Public Service – not Lip Service

For as long as I can remember, the beleaguered people of Macclesfield's large estates have been given assurances that everything is under control and that vandalism will be eliminated. Only recently, Nick Winterton wrote a well-meaning public letter saying that he had spoken with Senior Police Officers and now hoped that frightened and elderly residents felt 'reassured'. Well, of course, they don't feel 'reassured' Nick. They'll be 'reassured' when they can see uniformed policemen regularly walking past their front window, when they can go for a game of Bingo without worrying about leaving their homes and when they are no longer accosted by foul-mouthed louts on their way back.

If our politicians *really* want to know the way things are, stop asking the Top Brass and start talking to the workers at the coalface. Have a chat with the bobby on the beat who's trying to police the whole of Knutsford on his own on a Saturday night or talk to the local constable who has been told not to approach suspicious suspects in cars alone as he cannot be guaranteed any back up. These are the people who really do know what's happening and whose opinions we trust.

When my wife recently had a severe asthma attack at 12.30am, I dialled 999 and worried. The ambulance was there in minutes and the paramedics were brilliant, but my anxiety was further stimulated by the words 'Merseyside Health Authority' written on the side of the ambulance. I made a mental note to check my hubcaps later.

The staff at Macclesfield General were angels and soon had things under control and at 4am I finally left her in their capable hands and went home – the hubcaps *were* still intact. When I visited her again at 10am the following day I was astounded to find that she was still lying in the Accident and Emergency Area, nine and a half hours after being admitted. Apparently they were unable to find her a bed and I couldn't afford a private corridor.

Now I am not complaining but, if I was, I'm sure I would be 'reassured' by some Senior Manager with a well-rehearsed recital of Official Policy that would bring tears to a glass eye.

They would undoubtedly tell me that the number of patients remaining in the Accident and Emergency Area for nine hours expressed as a percentage of a Hospital Trust Managers salary was infinitesimal and forecast to be become even lower the next time they got a big pay increase. Therefore I'll save my breath and thank the people who really matter – the paramedics and nurses who were there when they were needed.

The next time that a scribbled letter from some frightened and vulnerable resident arrives at the Town Hall or at Conservative HQ do me a favour

— stay away from Top Management. Talk to a local bobby (if you can find one), speak to a nurse on the wards and ask them what the real situation is. Then do something about it! That way, there's a chance we may all get 're-assured'.

---

21 June 2000

The Sound of Silk

On my travels over the years, I have become aware that most towns have a unique and distinctive sound that defines the very essence of what they represent to the world. In Venice it's the magic of live Classical music ema-nating from the wonderful acoustics of Saint Mark's Square, in London it's the majestic chimes of Big Ben. New Orleans has the excitement of Mardi Gras and Paris the intimacy of the accordion. So, what does Macclesfield have? "Five for a pound your lighters. Six for a pound your Super Glue."

Makes you think doesn't it? Is this really the best effort we can muster? If that's the case then no wonder the town centre's dying. What town would want to be 'Twinned' with Macclesfield these days? The best chance we've got is a suicide pact with Tamworth.

What are our leaders doing about the sad state of our beloved town. Are they galvanised as one into a creative frenzy, burning the midnight oil in an effort to save our reputation while we still have one to save? As Del Boy would say "Au contraire".

Conservative Councillor Norman Edwards informs us that our Council spends so much time discussing at length matters over which they have absolutely no control (The Budget, Third World Debt, The Russian econ-omy ...) that when it comes to debating local issues "all we want to do is get the meeting finished and go home". Is this a frightening state of affairs or what?

Councillor Edwards is undoubtedly feeling somewhat peeved at his own Party for ousting him from his cherished Chairmanship of the East Area Planning Committee. His astounding admission could be construed as 'sour grapes' except for the fact that his damning comments concur exactly with those of Labour Leader Janet Jackson, hardly someone with whom he is likely to have compared notes.

Very recently, we've had the fiasco of Moss Rose where no one on the Council can agree what was discussed, when, by whom or why. Some councillors walked out of the meetings (always a brilliant way to keep informed) some said they only knew the details when they read about them in the Macclesfield Express and Coun. Brendan Murphy, Chairman Desig-nate of the Amenities and Recreation Committtee (nice title, Brendan) was astounded to know that a most important meeting had recently taken place between the Borough, the developers and Macclesfield Town Football Club from which he had been excluded.

We don't need a Town Hall, we need a Big Top. If these are the people to whom we have entrusted the future of our town then ... Bring on the Clowns.

It would actually be quite funny if it wasn't for the fact that while the boys and girls on the Council are playing 'Government and Opposition', the rest of us are picking up the tab. This is a new twist on 'Doctors and Nurses' — "I'll show you my development if you show me yours!" The rest of us are picking up the tab and our children and grandchildren will be paying for it years from now with grotesque, ill-conceived developments and hotch-potch schemes approved by a disinterested Council intent on playing Big Time Politics.

But all is not yet lost. We have a new Mayor, Coun. Walter Wright and — glory be — he's a farmer. Now, if anybody knows how many beans make five, it's a farmer. Lambs and calves don't hang around while you debate the future of the Euro.

So come on Walter — don't let them bog you down in all that handshaking, chain-rattling nonsense. Show 'em what a farmer can do and get the herd moving in the right direction. Put a few down if needs be. Take the whole damned lot to Chelford on a Monday if you must.

If there was ever a time that we needed a farmer in the Town Hall, this is it. Forget the mayoral chain, take a pitchfork and swing it like you mean business. Cajole them, embarrass them. Do what our American cousins describe as 'Kick Ass' — but save us from this shambles.

The following article, which appeared in July 2000, got me deep into the bad books of Coun. Ken Thompson. It resulted in him blasting me in a subsequent letter to The Express that caused me to be heckled around town for days. 'Good on ya Ken'.

28 June 2000

It Don't Mean A Thing

When 86 residents of Crompton Road signed a petition to support the alterations to the premises of a local car rental company and thus relieve their neighbourhood parking problems, Councillor Ken Thompson said "They'll sign anything (the residents) and I am inclined to say that these petitions don't mean anything."

So, presumably when the good people of Macclesfield South saw fit to put a cross against Councillor Thompson's name, that "didn't mean any-thing" either? In which case perhaps he'd like to close the door on his way out and make way for someone who actually thinks that their opinion is worth a damn.

I have no idea whether the alterations to the business concerned are a good idea or not but I'm sure as hell not going to rubbish the views of 86 local residents. Isn't that the real problem with our town?

The Council would rather spend five grand on outside consultants to tell them why the town centre is dying than listen to the people who actually work and shop there every day. We appear to have more than our share of councillors who have a listening problem. I heard a rumour the other day that the old Tesco in town is planning to close down and I raised the matter with an elderly councillor whom I met in Chestergate.

"Do you know what's happening with Tesco?" I inquired.

"You what?" he shouted.

"Tesco, what's happening?"

"You what?"

I really ramped up the decibels this time. "Tesco, do you know Tesco?"

"Well the last I heard England were all out for 238," came his eventual reply.

How does anyone qualify to be a councillor in Macclesfield anyway? Is there a medical where a doctor shines a torch down one ear and, if the light comes through onto the wall, you are automatically on the Council? Is that it?

I did ask one councillor, who has remained totally silent in the Council Chamber for his entire term of office, why he had not bothered to raise one single issue and he told me, quite honestly, that he was embarrassed to speak publicly because he has difficulty pronouncing his F's and his TH's.

Well, I don't suppose he can say fairer than that.

---

5 July 2000

Going Down

Indulge me, please. Do these sums with me. The Cheshire Population Report forecasts that the number of people living in Macclesfield is set to decline over the next three decades. OK? This being the case then the need for additional housing, retail premises and leisure complexes declines along with it. Agreed?

With a falling population, the priorities change from meeting the needs of expansion to improving the quality of the existing infrastructure. Yes?

So, why in God's name are the council fannying around with large new edge of town developments when the heart of our beloved town is going to hell on a handcart? On whose behalf are they acting?

Planning consent was given for a huge pub on the Silk Road near

Bollington. A major highway and a town that already has more pubs per head of population than blades of grass. How smart was that? If there was one damned thing we definitely didn't need in that precise location it was another pub.

This is not development to meet demand, this is development to *create* demand and the sort of thing done more appropriately in an underdeveloped area like the Arizona desert where land is not under pressure! Just what is going on, councillors?

Visit the town centre. Talk to local shopkeepers busting a gut to pay their bills and make a living. Walk along Chestergate, all the way along, don't stop at Churchill Way like the shoppers. Go down to the bottom end of Mill Street and ask yourself why Charity Shops have taken over once prime shopping sites.

We have retail businesses in town dying day by day. We have a declining population forecast and local families spending their cash out of town (where it is easier and cheaper to park) and we have a council with a desperate need of the income from all those business rates. You would have thought that such a convergence of interests would have concentrated the minds of those in the Town Hall.

So why the obsession with more out of town retail premises, more leisure centres, more super stores? more controversial housing developments? ... more ... more ... more?

There must be some huge benefits to be gained by pursuing such an illogical agenda but for whom?

It's high time that the people of Macclesfield found out!

---

5 July 2000

Brotherly Love

So Noel Gallagher of Oasis fame has abandoned the European Tour of his band and returned home saying he finds his even more famous brother Liam to be "obnoxious". He also adds that he is "sick of his brother's drunken behaviour". Well, Noel my boy, join the queue.

Unfortunately, this mode of conduct is not confined to moronic pop icons. As I write our so called 'football fans' are causing havoc in Belgium and there is talk of withdrawing their passports to prevent them travelling which I think is a wonderful idea provided it's done while they are away. Personally, I would rather have a plane-load of asylum seekers any day than get this lot back.

Just scan the stories that appear each week in the Macclesfield Express. 'Man left for Dead By Gang of Thugs', drunken street fights, disabled people robbed, defenceless old ladies mugged. Try walking down Park Lane in Poynton after eleven o'clock on a Friday or Saturday night. The place is awash with gangs of foul-mouthed drunken yobs roaming around the streets looking for trouble, as too is Macclesfield town centre. They are virtual No-Go areas for anyone not wanting a faceful of abuse.

So, why do we put up with it? The reaction of our Government to the criticism levied at it by UEFA following the deportation of British hooligans that "while we accept Europe's anger and frustration we do not accept that we are at fault" I think perhaps gives us a clue.

They, the Government, are not 'at fault'. The parents of these tattooed mutants are certainly not 'at fault' and Heaven forbid that the thugs themselves are held to be 'at fault'. In fact no one is 'at fault' and if anyone is 'at fault' it's probably the wicked Belgian policemen. Just like it was the Turkish policemen and French policemen before them.

Have a look at the sentences passed out by local magistrates in the Macclesfield Express — probation, small fines and community service seem to be the order of the day. For more serious offences sentences are usually 'deferred pending social/psychiatric reports'.

What has been the most effective new law in the last twenty years? The answer of course is the Drink Driving Legislation. It has changed all our attitudes and why? If you offend, there are no social/psychiatric reports, no 'I am not responsible' nonsense, no trendy 'three strikes and you're out' baloney. We all know in advance what the penalty is and it works.

Last week's heartbreaking lead story in the Macclesfield Express concerned the knife attack on a poor defenceless Shetland Pony at Higher Fence Farm. Why anyone would want to inflict such pain on a horse is beyond me. How do you defend a little pony grazing out in a field? Do you hire a private army? Should you have to?

The week before we had morons pulling down the band stand and trampling the marquee at a fête held for the benefit of the terminally ill. If they are ever apprehended, what's the betting it will be 'community service' or 'social reports'? Last year a youth failed to turn up for *any* of his 100 hours community service and so magistrates doubled it. How stupid is that? No wonder the police despair.

If I read once more about the 'underprivileged' background of any of these hooligans I swear I'll vomit over the nearest magistrate. If ever anyone was 'underprivileged' it's the 75 pence a week pensioners and hard-pressed mothers trying to juggle full time jobs, kids, shopping, laundry, mortgages.

When did you last hear about a foul-mouthed gang of pensioners smashing shop windows or working mothers wrecking the hopes of the terminally ill? You can bet your life if they did they'd get the book thrown at them. No chance of 'social reports' here.

So what's going on? 'The Emperor's New Clothes' — that's what's going on. Trendy social workers and gutless magistrates have been telling us for years that these thugs are the 'underprivileged expressing their frustration with an unsympathetic society'. Take a good look around you at the heart-break and misery they cause. They are not 'underprivileged', they are evil people with evil intent respecting nothing and no one and proud of it.

So, next time a householder gets into trouble for defending his home against criminals or a hard pressed headteacher expels a foul-mouthed child or a conscientious local bobby gets suspended for carrying out his unfashionable, non-Politically Correct duty get behind them. Give them your support. Write letters, complain, start a petition, make your voice heard, stand up for what you really believe in. Strike a blow for the Victims like that little defenceless Shetland pony and all those patients at the East Cheshire Hospice who cannot do it for themselves.

Our worst enemy is our own silence.

12 July 2000

Hearts & Minds

In view of my regular comments on the local political scene I have been questioned several times lately on the nature of my own politics. Please allow me to expand.

My entire formative years were spent as a member of a staunch social-ist household, in a marginal Labour ward of Greater Manchester, with a father who, for thirty-two years, was a devoted Union Secretary. Naturally, I grew up believing the Labour Party to be the only possible choice for the likes of me and my family until one apocalyptic day, when a heated political argument within our neighbourhood forced me to recall exactly what the local Labour Party had done for us during the first 18 years of my life.

To my acute embarrassment I discovered that the only thing I could think of was a bus shelter built outside our house that actually faced the wrong way so that, when the bus arrived, it was actually behind you. People alighting from the bus were so confused that many of them, believ-ing that they had actually been queuing in the shelter, got back on again.

This was the 1960s when the Tories owned everything and wanted to keep it to themselves and the Socialists had nothing and wanted to share it with everyone. So I was persuaded by trendy pals to try the Liberals, as they were then known and all went swimmingly until the day they actually gained control of our ward.

At this time we were desperate for a pedestrian crossing and street lights. What did we get? A permanent camp site for gypsies. No one in our area had ever seen a gypsy before then. There weren't a lot of fruit crops to be picked in Manchester during the sixties. Nevertheless, a gypsy camp is what we got. No doubt, Liberal politicians of the day would have argued, not unreasonably, that what we lost in maimed pedestrians we more than made up for in clothes pegs.

Finally, I turned my attention to the Tories. On the basis that they could do no worse. I threw my lot in with the 'Toffs' as my father scathingly referred to them. With energy and enthusiasm known only to the young I became 'Tory Boy' and sported a blue rosette, knocked on doors, can-vassed and generally embarrassed my family. With the aid of a Tory Gov-ernment and a bit of gerrymandering the Local Conservatives eventually gained control. I was overjoyed, vindicated   ... but not for long.

Along with other wide sweeping changes to our town they decided to introduce numerous one-way systems one of which included our street, unfortunately failing to realise that it was a cul-de-sac. Within hours of its introduction, we had 90% of the entire traffic flow of Greater Manchester corralled outside our house.

It was around this time that Ted Heath went head to head with the miners and had to put everyone on a three-day week. Men in our neighbourhood were furious, most of them had only ever worked two. So it was against this background of disappointment and disillusionment with politicians in general and the idiotic incompetence of Town Hall mandarins in particular that I came to live in Macclesfield.

Ladies and Gentlemen ... I rest my case.

12 July 2000

Asylum Silkers

Imagine the scene. The year is 2011. The Place: Market Square, Bukhoro, Uzbekistan. A lorry driver opens the rear door of his truck and from beneath the tons of raw vegetables he hears the weak but unmistakable sound of human voices.

He calls the local militia. They surround his vehicle with uniformed officers, Kalashnikovs at the ready. The stowaways are ordered out of the vehicle. A bedraggled and pitiful group of men and women stumble from beneath the truck's rotting load and stand nervously while policemen strip search them, demanding to see their papers.

"We request political asylum," screams the leader of the group. "We are from England."

"We do not offer asylum to peoples from Western Europe," replies the Senior Officer, "you have wealth and shelter and food enough of your own."

"Yeah, I know, but we're all from Macclesfield."

"Ah, then of course, come share our sheep's giblets with us."

"What are sheep, Stan?" asks one of the refugees of his leader.

"They're what we used to have around Macclesfield before the Council poured concrete on every blade of grass, remember?"

"And who is your Council?" barks the interrogator.

"Jones Homes."

"This is a very strange name for a Town Council is it not?" he asks suspiciously.

"Well they used to be called 'Macclesfield Council' but they got overthrown in a bloodless coup."

"And why do you wish to leave your town?"

"Well we didn't actually want to leave. We were in the town centre looking for a parking space and this was as near as we could get."

"But why would you want to settle here in Bukhoro where our once bustling market square is a bleak windswept area of desolation, the politicians inept, the developers all corrupt and no-one gives a damn about the views of ordinary people?"

"Go on you tell him, Stan."
"We're home sick."
You think it couldn't happen? If the mental midgets in the Town Hall continue to neglect the infrastructure of our once proud town centre while encouraging tasteless theme pubs and dubious out-of-town, land-grabbing, developments Uzbekhistan may start to look like Paradise to our grandchildren.

---

19 July 2000

Big Brother

Hi Folks, sshhhh ... keep the noise down. Just look over your shoulder and make sure there's no one around from the Town Hall. If there is then go into the loo and lock the door. I want to talk to you in private this week.

If you're reading this in public hold the paper up high so that no one can recognise you. OK, if you've already started reading stay with me on this ... it's like taking antibiotics: you have to finish the course to see the result.

Have you been watching Big Brother on Channel Four? Sshhhh keep it down. Whisper. Well, this is a programme in which ten egocentric young members of the public have been willingly locked up in a remote building with over 200 microphones and cameras installed to record their every deed. Is it my imagination, or did they all have their kit off within five minutes of meeting each other?

Anyway they have no radios, phones, newspapers or TV, in fact no contact with the outside world whatsoever – only interaction between themselves and an intercom to 'Big Brother'. The whole thing is being pumped out live on the Internet 24 hours a day and you can watch 'selected highlights' – whatever they are – nightly on Channel Four.

Each week, the public vote to have one of the internees evicted from the building and the last one remaining receives £70k. But the real attraction to these born exhibitionists is the opportunity for national recognition and stardom.

So, are you ready? SShhhhhh! Have a quick look around. OK? I've got a Secret Plan. Given the enormous love of publicity some of our councillors have, I thought we might lure the entire Macclesfield Borough Council into volunteering for the very same 'Big Brother' type idea.

We incarcerate them all in a remote, unpopular, purpose-built location, where no one will ever find them. Like the Millennium Dome, but instead of being equipped with over 200 microphones and cameras this one will have no microphones and no cameras (but we don't tell'em!)

I quietly floated the idea past a few shoppers around town, and some suggested that it should also have no *air*. Maxonians can be so wicked.

It's become obvious that our chances of getting a cinema or anything else that *we* actually want or need from the present system is next to zero, so it's up to us to make a change and this is our best opportunity yet.

Every Council Committee is made up of dozens of councillors − 32 on the Planning Committee. They squabble like children and, when they're not squabbling, they are working out why things can't be done. It's what child psychologists call developing 'no can do' attitude and they're damned good at it.

Now we obviously don't need to have 32 councillors knocking good ideas around until they emerge as a pale shadow of their former selves. What we really need is one good Councillor who actually knows a sensible idea when he sees one and can make a decision and I know just the person. The Mayor.

He's no publicity-seeking pseudo MP. He's a farmer, totally committed to Macclesfield and if he's still got a farm to run after this Government's ignorance and persecution of all things rural then he must be tough as old boots. So here's what we do ...

Every week, when we vote for who to let out of our secure, remote building, we always vote for the Mayor. Simple when you think about it isn't it? We just keep telling the rest of them how much publicity they're getting and they'll be happy as Larry. If we say that we're trying to find them a 'safe seat' in Westminster most of them will stay in there forever. Lovely Jubbly!

Meanwhile, the Mayor knocks up a cinema at Lyme Green, tells all the developers who seem to hang around Macclesfield like blood-sucking leeches that, for their money-spinning plans to be considered, they must first serve 10 years on the beat as a Macclesfield Constable without pay. Then the Mayor makes everything outside the town centre part of the Green Belt. Next he moves his livestock into the council chamber so that he can hold a sensible conversation whenever the mood takes him and ... Hey, Presto! Everyone's a winner!

Are you all with me? OK, let's do it.

---

26 July 2000

My Hero

Ladies and gentlemen, please have a pen or pencil ready. I am about to give you an important name. Ready? 'Paul Sims'. This guy is my hero and he should be yours too.

He is the manager of Alldays Store on Buxton Road and has to continually deal with shoplifters, drunks and ignorant louts who steal, make threats and cause a nuisance in his shop. So, when he was recently confronted with a known thief whom he had previously banned from the store he asked him to leave.

The man in question refused to accept the ban and threw sweets onto the floor of the shop, whereupon Mr Sims pushed him out of the door. Unfortunately, the unwelcome customer tripped and hit his head on the door handle and subsequently prosecuted Mr Sims who was ... wait for it ... "ordered to pay the victim £50".

Mr Sims says that "In the past the police have not pressed charges against shoplifters because the items taken have been too small". They would be – it's a sweet shop. He has senior management who, not unreasonably, expect him to be responsible for the stock in his store. At the same time, he says that he has met total indifference from the police.

He is a family man with four children to support, so what's he supposed to do? Lose his stock and his job? He did what any responsible manager would and ejected a known thief who had already been barred from the premises. Now he's the one with the tarnished reputation which will no doubt follow him throughout his career.

What message are the magistrates trying to send out? "Behave like a moron and we will support you. Defend your premises and we'll convict you?" Can any sane person see any sense in this at all? Given the appalling judgement of our magistrates and the proliferation of foul-mouthed mutants in our community it's a wonder we can find anyone to run a pub or shop at all.

So I've decided that as far as I personally am concerned it's 'stand up and be counted' time and I have a cheque for £5 on its way to Mr Sims right now. I'm damned if I am going to let a hard-working young guy be penalised for trying to run an orderly business. There are far too many wimps around telling us all to lie down and let these abusive louts walk all over us.

If you feel as I do that Paul Sims has been badly treated drop him a line. I know from the many letters you send me that Macclesfield people are pretty good at putting pen to paper so lend him your support or just call in at the shop. He would undoubtedly appreciate it. Send him a quid or, if you can't afford it twenty pence, anything that will show him where you stand.

Next time it could be you who is being abused and you'll be looking around and hoping that a guy like Paul Sims is brave and decent enough to help you out. Here's his address:

Paul Sims, Alldays, Buxton Road, Macclesfield

May the force Be With You!

2 August 2000

Whining For Europe

Until recently, I never knew who Chris Davies was, but I do now. He's our Euro MP. He's been in every local paper I've read recently and he sounds like a real whinger. He's upset at receiving letters of dissent from 'nutters'. Well let me tell you something Chris, the people of Macclesfield are fed up of being represented by them.

Go get yourself a job working behind the bar in a local pub or on the A&E ward of Macclesfield General or perhaps accompany one of our local bobbies around town on a Saturday night then you might just get an idea what dealing with 'nutters' is really about.

You see Chris there's one little element you seem to be missing out here, i.e. all these people being abused by drunks, dressing blood-soaked wounds and putting their necks on the line to uphold law and order are doing it for the sort of money you wouldn't get out of bed for.

So, you will forgive them won't you if they appear to be a little less sympathetic than you would wish but for a lot of them the sort of aggravation you are complaining of is a daily occurrence.

Have a word with Mrs B and ask her the price she has to pay for my weekly input into the Macclesfield Express. She can hardly get past the Cheshire Gap (it's a shop Chris) without someone telling her how disgusted they were at my discussing her underwear in public or asking her what am I going to do about gamma rays from Jodrell Bank blighting their rhubarb? It's the price you pay for doing the job.

I think you would agree that the European Parliament has not presented itself in the best possible manner and whilst we all realise that having a wider trading base and lower tariffs are great ideas, having our farming industry decimated and our legal system undermined are not. Add to that the level of corruption in the highest echelons, the outrageous expense of the whole operation and you will begin to see why bankrupt farmers and massively overworked nurses might just think that your job is a piece of cake. You have a very good salary, generous expenses, luxurious working conditions and not one penny of your own money at risk.

A really smart guy might consider this the right time to quit whining and get on with the task at hand.

---

2 August 2000

Last Bus To Clarksville

I have been helping organise a party in Macclesfield town centre for next Wednesday evening and I was given the job of checking on late night buses to various locations. A simple task I thought at the time. I let my fingers do the walking and found Arriva's number in the Yellow pages but when I called it, a recorded message told me it was incorrect and I had to dial another number.

That number proved to be engaged so it was some time before I was able to talk to the bus company who then told me to my utter amazement that the last bus to Rainow was quarter past six. The same to Henbury was nine-thirty and there were no buses to Chelford or Bosley at all. While I had his attention, I asked him about services to Sutton on August Bank Holiday Monday and he informed me they would be the same as a 'normal Sunday'.

"OK, so what's a normal Sunday?" I inquired.

"Just a minute I'll look it up." Another ten-minute wait while I bristled and then he gave me the stunning answer. "None at all."

He proffered a Macclesfield telephone number for Cheshire Bus Services and I asked them how we would get people home to Bosley and Chelford late at night. I could hear him talking to other people around him.

"We're just trying to find Chelford," he said, in an attempt to keep me informed.

"Trying to find Chelford? You are a Macclesfield bus company for goodness sake, surely you can find Chelford!" I responded doing a fair impression of Victor Meldrew.

"No we're not."

"Not what?" I demanded.

"A Macclesfield bus company."

"Well what are you then?"

"We're a Call Centre at Ellesmere Port."

So, to find out if there was a bus to Bosley or Chelford I had to call a Macclesfield telephone number to talk to someone in Ellesmere Port who had never heard of either. Does this make sense to anybody?

The bottom line is that a Bakers Coach leaves Macclesfield for Chelford at 5.45pm, two hours before the party is due to start.

So, the next time you cast your vote at a local election, it just might be a good idea to find out if the councillor for whom you are voting has any idea or any interest in finding out how anyone unfortunate enough to be stuck in Macclesfield after tea time and without a car is going to get home.

Pity the poor people of Sutton if they are late finishing their shopping — they can't get home until Monday.

---

9 August 2000

Coronation Copy Cat

What exactly is going on in Coronation Street? Supermarket trolleys keep appearing outside our house and middle-aged ladies are stopping me in the street and asking how Deirdre is getting on? Am I missing something here?

Then I started receiving phone calls asking me if my book was going to be as good as Ken Barlow's? I tried saying "Oh Rita, I don't rightly know," but they still keep calling. I thought Ken Barlow died after he was attacked by Minnie Caldwell's cat or was he run over by a tram? Maybe he was the taxi driver with one foot, who went mad after his wife had lip implants and retired to a convent?

No, just a minute, don't tell me. Ken Barlow? Mmm ... let me see now ... isn't he the drug dealer that just killed the son of the landlady at the Rovers Return and then got off with it?

Quite honestly, I have no idea what's going on in Coronation Street or what the content of Ken Barlow's book is going to be. But of one thing you can be sure whatever material he's had in Weatherfield to write about, it's nowhere near as good as I've had living in Macclesfield for thirty years.

Weatherfield may well be the most dangerous town in Britain but Macclesfield is definitely the funniest. Where else in the world would you have an 'Open Day' at the Crematorium as we did a couple of years ago? What other town would renovate its market square at huge expense and then hold its market on a car park? Name anywhere on God's Earth that has a bypass that actually doesn't lead to anywhere or a town the size of ours with less cinemas and more pubs? It can't be done.

So, sorry Ken. I wish you every success with your book but when you compare Weatherfield with the goings on in Macclesfield you don't really stand a chance.

---

9 June 2000

Err ... What's Up Doc?

I was in town recently and called in at the doctor's surgery and asked to make an appointment. "Is it urgent?" the receptionist asked testily.

"Not really,"I replied, "but my wife has arranged a severe case of gastroenteritis for me next Wednesday, as a birthday treat, so anytime around then would be great."

My attempt at humour was ignored. "Who is your doctor?" she demanded without looking up from her computer.

Well, to be honest, in the few years since I have been at this particular surgery I have seen so many different doctors that I never realised that one of them was actually 'mine'. Had I known I would have insisted on him 'living in'.

"I suppose I'll have to check your records," she grumbled.

Now, I don't know what she saw on her computer screen but whatever it was was not good.

"You can see the nurse right away," she said hastily. "Up the front stairs, across the landing, down a flight, first door on the left."

"But I don't want to see the nurse," I remonstrated, "I want to see a doctor, *my* doctor, you know the grumpy one who never looks you in the eye, with bad breath." It was too late – she was already grilling her next victim.

I took off in the direction of The Nurse's Den. Up the stairs, down the stairs, first door on the left ... I walked straight into a bathroom where a young mother was breast feeding her baby. "Ooops, sorry," I stammered, "I'm just nippling in to see the nurse," I stuttered, red faced with embarrassment.

"Oh, that's OK," she replied calmly, "it's across the landing down the other stairs."

"Oh right, thanks. I breast be off then," and I retreated before I made an even bigger fool of myself.

I found the Nurse's Room where I just wanted to explain the mistake but I had to sit outside in the corridor with a group of patients whose average age must have been around 90.

"Do you want some dog fat for rubbing!" an ancient guy sitting next to me suddenly bellowed.

"No thanks," I responded when the ringing in my ears subsided.

"Best thing you can have is dog fat." I nodded warily just in case he was about to whip the donating mongrel out of his trousers.

"Goose grease," yelled a lady farther down the line, "Take no notice of him love. You want to use goose grease."

Dog fat, goose grease – what was going on here? Whatever it was they were advocating I was not going to find it at Body Shop.

Thankfully at that point the door opened and the nurse herself came out.

"Now is anyone here allergic to eggs?"she inquired.

"I don't like 'em boiled," said Methuselah.

The nurse nodded kindly and said that this was OK and retreated back to her office with Mrs Goose Grease. I picked up a magazine and caught up on the latest news regarding Labour's stunning 1997 election victory. Dog Fat was just about to launch into another of his Remedies from Hell when the nurse called out "Mr Barlow" and I sprinted for sanctuary.

"I shouldn't be here," I explained breathlessly as she rolled up my sleeve"

"Were you intending to leave earlier?" she inquired routinely fiddling with something behind my back.

"Yeah, I was actually, but I thought I should at least see you first."

"And very important that you did," she said simultaneously pricking my arm with a small syringe. "There, now that should do it. You may find that you feel quite nauseous. You might even vomit but it's quite normal. After the swelling dies down you should be fine. If you're not you should see a doctor."

Nauseous? Vomit? Swelling? I was about to tell her that a doctor was *exactly* what I had come to see when she ushered me to the door and shouted "Next!" My records had apparently been confused with another Mr Barlow who by now was on his way up the Orinoco on a Saga Holiday blissfully unaware that all he had to protect him from the ravishes of a billion South American insects was my Pile Ointment. While I, on the other hand, had enough bacterial antibodies in my system to enable me to hike naked around the equator with complete immunity when all I had planned was a game of tennis in South Park as soon as the pain from my haemorrhoids subsided.

16 August 2000

Pussy Cat, Pussy Cat

Have you driven through Broken Cross recently? Isn't it a pig? You could learn to play 'Flight of The Bumble Bee' down the spout of a kettle while you are waiting to get to the Cross.

The contractors seem to work only a few hours a day and even then not every day. Our illustrious Council explain this away by saying that the contractor concerned has 'taken on too much work'. Aw! Poor love. Did-Ums!

On returning home from holiday I noticed a sign on London Road stating 'Works start here for 4 weeks July 31st'. So, this week I decided to skip London Road and go home via Byrons Lane and — guess what? Yep, they're digging up Byrons Lane again, just a few short weeks after it was excavated for two whole months. It gets better. When I went out to the leisure centre later in the evening I decided I would risk the London Road route rather than be stuck again at the 'temporary lights' on Byrons Lane. This was a brilliant decision because it was six o'clock in the evening and the entire road works had clocked off for the day. They had at least three more hours of daylight left and they had all packed up and gone home.

What sort of Mickey Mouse organisation is our Town Hall running? When I worked for a company that supplied clothing to 400 plus retailers across Europe we had various categories of customers.

We had the professionals who negotiated so hard that they tied us down on every detail of their order and were so demanding that if we failed to meet their exacting requirements we were penalised. They monitored everything and accepted no excuses whatsoever. These customers wanted decisions and immediate action and could only be serviced by one of our senior directors.

Then we had other customers who paid very little attention to detail and who were happy to leave everything to us rather than have the hassle of keeping on top of things and if we short delivered or were late they never seemed to notice. These retailers could be serviced by anyone, it didn't matter, as most of the time they never knew what was occurring until long after the event.

Just what sort of customer do you think Macclesfield Borough Council is? Surely we must have some clout in the contracting industry or is the civil engineering business so under supplied that we have to accept any slap-dash working practises that contractors care to operate.

Get a grip councillors and stop pussy-footing around with these companies. Insist as part of the contract that they should maximise daylight working and that the job should be completed by a set date and hit them with severe penalty clauses if they fail to deliver. Accept no excuses. If you can't find Officers prepared to toughen up recruit some that can.

Co-ordinate the various works so that local businesses are not penalised over and over again when the same stretch of road is continually disrupted. Yes, we know that some works are emergencies and have to be dealt with as such, but don't make it an excuse for weak, sloppy supervision.

Get some bite and stand up for the Borough of Macclesfield. Let's get ourselves a reputation for tough, fair dealing with no excuses accepted. You will be very unpopular with the regular contractors for a while but the people of Macclesfield will love you for it.

Let the contractors who don't like it go find some other pussy-cat Council and let's have some new suppliers who are hungry for our business and who treat the Borough of Macclesfield with the respect we deserve.

Oh yeah and one other thing. Don't debate it to death. As that famous sports brand says: "Just Do It!".

---

16 August 2000

Our Man Nick

Last weekend I attended the musical extravaganza following the Sutton Sheep Dog Trials. John Downes was, as usual, an excellent compère. We had terrific singing, irreverent comedy, hot burgers and cold beer, all in all a great night. Then Nick Winterton arrived and I have to admit my blood ran cold and I needed to be physically supported by Mrs B.

Since the day I arrived in Macclesfield this man has dogged my footsteps (if you'll pardon the pun). He's been at every fête I have ever attended. He turns up at obscure parties where I wouldn't have expected him, he goes to christenings of babies that he doesn't know and funerals of people that he does. He opens things that need opening and closes things that don't. He's sat at the front of every amateur drama production I was ever in and when I was persuaded to run in the Rainow Fell Race he turned out to be the Starter. Oh how I longed for that pistol to fire more than blanks! But I know that shooting him wouldn't work. He is omnipresent. I am sure that there are dozens of him. There have to be, he's everywhere.

Sometimes I wake up screaming in the middle of the night certain that he's about to get into bed between me and Mrs B! Now here he was, in my village again! I was not a happy bunny and I told anyone prepared to listen. "He's way past his sell-by date." I opined. Then he jumped up and spoke and I just knew he was going to be around for another twenty years.

He was robust, witty, appreciative and colourful. He thanked the people for coming, the organisers for organising and the singers for singing. He thanked the shepherds for whistling and given half a chance would have thanked each sheep and dog personally and do you know something? Had he done so they'd have voted for him as well. Let's face it he may have spent half his entire life stalking me but he is a brilliant, hard-working MP and I would never like to be the prospective candidate running against him.

Whatever else he might be Nick is absolutely sincere and therein lies his political Achilles heel. You never get anywhere in politics being sincere, see President Clinton for details. So I'm sorry Nick – while your idiot of a leader is trying to persuade everyone that he used to drink 14 pints of beer a day and 'Tony of the Satanic Smile' is preaching a fairer and just Britain while knifing pensioners in the back, your kind of sincerity is never going to make it. In my humble opinion Nick I think I have more chance of succeeding to the throne than you have of becoming 'Mr. Speaker'. But anytime you're stuck for a bed ...

---

23 August 2000

Discipline

When I was a young kid it was quite fashionable to receive a whack off your parents for stepping out of line. They were never to learn of the advantages to be gained from allowing us to do drugs and run wild. Unfortunately the act of spanking me caused my father to have amnesia and on or around the third smack to my legs would ask "Who do you think you are?" There would follow another smack then he would forget who he was and ask "Who do you think I am?"

Finally towards the end of the thrashing he would lose his hearing as well and want to know "Who do you think you are talking to?" I, of course, would cry profusely and sob "I'll never do it again dad, honest", as was the customary response. Then I would join my pals back on the street (some of whom had just undergone the same ritual or had been pre-smacked to save time) to carry on with whatever we were doing in the first place.

Having exercised all the various stages of chastisement to no avail my father always then reverted to a very clever psychological ploy guaranteed to get a result. He would tell me to do *exactly* the opposite of whatever he wanted me to do. This challenge stopped me in my tracks and I felt duty bound to prove I could ignore him and, as a result, ended up doing what he wanted.

So this week we are going to try this on the Borough Council ...

Don't build us a multiplex cinema in Lyme Green.

Do have road-works that go on forever.

Do get those Crosby homes knocked up in Jacksons Lane, Kerridge.

And try **not** to get your head stuck in heavy machinery.

---

23 August 2000

Summer Games

The weather has been great. It's summer, everyone's in holiday spirit so lets have some fun this week. First off let's try a couple of conundrums:

What have a new housing development in Kerridge and industrial units in Albert Road in Bollington got in common?

Answer: We don't want either but we are going to get both.

Next question: Why is a town centre market and a bobby on the beat like the Taj Mahal and Julia Roberts?

Answer: You won't find any of them in Macclesfield

If you are reading this at work and the boss is getting on your wick take a break and try this little teaser. Name half a dozen things that people in Macclesfield really want. For example:

☞ Abolition of parking charges in the town centre.

☞ A freeze on new industrial sites.

☞ Renovation of the town centre.

☞ Ability to call Macclesfield Police Station direct.

Then take away the one you first thought of and write the remainder on a blank piece of paper. Write some in ink and some in pencil (Block Capitals only). Fold the paper into four exact quarters and tear carefully across the folds. Go for a walk around town and drop all four pieces of paper down a grid.

And that's how much chance you have of getting anything you wrote down.

Here's a good one – try this.

You are a member of the Cabinet (pick a Party: it doesn't matter which) and you have ready access to an enormous fund of public money. You want to use it to create a landmark for the millennium.

Do you:

a) Build State of the Art hospitals in every region that are the envy of Europe?

b) Erect a grotesque edifice in the Capital that makes your country (and party) the laughing stock of the world?

c) Wait until you see the final outcome and take credit for any success while disassociating yourself from any failure?

How did you rate?

Check your answers against the following:

a) Yes? You are totally unsuitable for political life.

b) Yes? You have the natural talent to be a politician.

c) Yes? You are destined for high political office.

Right, time to try a spot of mental arithmetic.

The Government builds a Dome with £750m of your money.
They sell it to the Japanese seven months later for £105m.
Then give £53m of the £105m back.
How much money have they made for you?

And finally:

If it takes 60 Macclesfield Councillors 12 months to build 5 pubs we don't need, how long does it take them to build a multiplex cinema we do need?

OK. Back to business. Personally I'm fed up with local councillors complaining that only three out of ten voters bothered to turn out at the local elections. When you read Ken Thompson's article in last week's Macclesfield Express regarding the scheming within his own Council chamber that prevented us from having a multiplex at Lyme Green you begin to get an understanding of why seven out of ten Maxonians think that casting their vote is a waste of time.

More questionable is the manipulative way in which council members were prevented from meeting with the District Auditor regarding the town's finances. The Auditor, whose job it is to scrutinise the financial dealings of Councils throughout the North West, was invited to attend the relevant Policy Meeting held to discuss her report on the actual day that the meet-

ing took place. It doesn't take a genius to know that her chances of drop-
ping everything to race over to Macclesfield were zero.

You would have thought that the Council might want its members to talk
directly to the author of such an important report but apparently not. In fact
from his comments reported in the Macclesfield Express, Coun. Brendan
Murphy seems to think it an extremely bad idea. I wonder why?

Not long ago we had the very experienced Conservative Coun.
Norman Edwards telling us all how divisive and shambolic he considers
council meetings to be. None of us needs reminding of the debacle that
was the Southern Area Development Committee.

This is not a very impressive track record. Unspecified developments
that may or may not include a football stadium, important auditors reports
discussed without access to the author and a desperately needed cinema
not even in the planning stage.

Think about it ... SIXTY Macclesfield Councillors sat in that chamber
and they couldn't get a small multiplex cinema built in three years. If they
had put their minds to it they could have all gone down to Lyme Green and
built one themselves in a couple of days. So councillors the floor is yours.
What exactly is going on? Surely a small multiplex cinema and a public
report of a direct discussion with our town's financial watchdog is not too
much to ask?

---

30 August 2000

Litre Beaters

The price of petrol now means that some weeks Mrs B and I have to go
without victuals in order to fill up the Hillman Minx. Consequently, I have
become a lot more aware of exactly how much I'm paying at the pump. I
may have been duped by the change over from good old gallons to
Euro-friendly litres but not any more. No Sir!

I used to just stick in twenty quid's worth but suddenly found myself running out of petrol before I made it through Stockport. So I started compar-
ing prices. What a shock! Just like Victor Meldrew, 'I couldn't believe it!'

It didn't matter which direction I went out of Macclesfield, the price of
petrol was at least 2 pence cheaper and sometimes 5 pence — that's
almost 23 pence a gallon! Surely, there was some mistake. It couldn't be
that, for all these years, filling stations in Macclesfield have been over-
charging me could it?

I'd already gone to Congleton and explained the cheaper fuel there to
myself by saying that 'it's on the way to a major Motorway.' Stockport was a
'high volume commuter corridor' I told myself and Manchester was
cheaper because it was a 'big city'.

This kept the nagging voices from suggesting that I'd been had big style until I went through Leek (nobody goes *to* Leek) and found that I could save at least 2 pence a litre there. In Leek! There's only antique shops and sheep there. Oh yeah, and maybe some honest filling station operators.

So, if you don't want to be ripped off, starve them of business until you get value for money. Fill up your car anywhere but in Macc and you'll save ££££££s!

---

30 August 2000

Football Crazy

I read recently that the padre of the French national football team prayed that when his team of eleven millionaires were losing one nil to Italy in Euro 2000 that they would score a last-minute equaliser and win with a 'Golden Goal' in extra time. They did exactly that.

Given all the pain and suffering in the world wouldn't you think he just might have offered a few words towards the ending of world famine, the termination of war and a cure for all crippling diseases? That is, only if his soccer duties weren't too pressing of course.

---

6 September 2000

Happiness

Just imagine my predicament, I'm sitting in my office staring at the computer screen. I have this week's column to write and just for once I'm totally stuck for words. Never happened before, ever. The Council has disappeared for the summer and I'm really missing them more than I ever thought possible. Macclesfield Police are at last getting some additional bobbies, so no material there. Nobody has written to say how 'scurrilous' I am for two whole weeks and owners everywhere appear to be cleaning up after their dogs. It's just awful.

I make another cup of Earl Grey and start slowly head butting the screen. The phone rings – it could be someone letting me know that Nick Winterton has had a sex change. What a story!

But instead it's James Tute from the Macclesfield Express office positively crackling with tension.

"Suppose you know Pat Hills (News Editor) is away all week?" he jabbered.

"Yeah, well I, er ... "

"Look Vic, I'm holding the fort so you better have something up your sleeve. I need a really good piece from you this week." And, before I could let him know just how little I actually had, he was gone ... lunging up the corporate ladder, headlong towards an impossible deadline. I put my hands to my face and heaved a heavy sigh for my amateur inability to deliver the goods in my young colleague's hour of need.

The phone rang again: "Yes James, I'm working on it. I'm working on it." It went silent for a second.

"Is that Vic Barlow?"

"Yeah, this is me. Who's that?"

"It's Ken Dodd here."

"Ken who?"

"Dodd, you know Doddy."

"Yeah right, and I'm married to Michelle Pfeiffer."

"No it is. It's me, Ken Dodd. What's all this I hear about you writing in the Macclesfield Express?"

It *was* Doddy. The man himself calling me in response to a request I made at the Bollington Festival for an interview. I did consider asking him to say, "Are you tickled Mrs?" just by way of identification but it proved unnecessary.

I knew he wasn't over keen to do interviews and had recently refused a couple of the nationals but he knows the people in these parts adore him and so here he was talking to them via me and the Macclesfield Express. Now I know this is not the sort of journalism that would impress Kate Adie, but I really wanted to make the most it.

I asked him how he got started and he said his father loved comedians and took him to the theatre regularly when he was a child and he became stage-struck. He bought a ventriloquist's dummy and gave shows to other children in his back garden. (I wondered what time these kids got home?)

I asked, tongue in cheek, how he thought the audience at the Bollington Festival compared with that at the London Palladium and he said that jokes he told us in Bollington never got a laugh at the Palladium. I stupidly asked why.

"They can't hear them."

We discussed his favourite music. It was 'Happiness'. I should have known better. Obviously, it wasn't going to be Black Sabbath. Oh yes →and he loves Handel's Largo; apparently he wouldn't drink anything else.

Ken's an avid reader and his greatest extravagance is his library of over 20,000 books on theatre and showbiz topics all of which he says he's read and I believe him. He hates bullies and violent behaviour of any kind and thinks that respect for others and honesty are the essential qualities of life.

I asked him about his off duty time and where, if anywhere, he goes on holiday but he wouldn't answer. He also declined my invitation to enter into a witty exchange at the expense of our beloved Council. I told him that they'd understand and enjoy the publicity but he said he didn't want to 'hurt anyone'. It was clear that he is uncomfortable discussing Ken Dodd the person — probably because his entire world is up there on stage for all to see. He's been entertaining us for 45 years. It's all he wants to do. When I asked him what his favourite weekend would be, he said, "Being warmly welcomed onto the stage of a beautiful theatre and making 'em laugh."

Ken Dodd: comedy genius

He's made dozens of TV specials, appeared in front of the Queen more often than Charles, starred at the London Palladium year after year and totally dominated seaside comedy for decades and still he's prepared to appear in a tent at Bollington. Just to make us laugh.

I asked from where he was calling, expecting him to be at Granada Television or some city centre hotel but instead he said simply, "I'm in the kitchen, at home". The same home in which he was born and yes, he really does live in Knotty Ash. He meant to turn on the toaster while he was talking to me but instead switched on the TV. He's obviously not handy around the house and is it any wonder? He's spent his entire adult life 'on tour'.

Once comedians make a name, they generally pursue wider ambitions and leave the smaller venues behind while they attempt to break into TV acting, presenting or hosting game shows — but not Doddy. It never happened. He never wanted it to happen. The moment he heard his first audience laugh he was hooked. He became an addict and it's dominated his entire life.

When excited families squash into early morning taxis heading for the airport and the wonders of Disney, Ken packs up his well-travelled suitcase and drives himself to the next gig, the next town and his next Happiness Show. When friends and neighbours party the night away in homes bedecked with holly and mistletoe, Doddy grabs his tickling stick, and puts Dicky Mint—his ventriloquist's dummy—in the back of the car, ready to add another 1000 lonely miles to the 100,000 he travels each year in pursuit of laughter.

There are no annual holidays to agonise over in Ken's house, no grandchildren to ruin, no wife with whom to plan a leisure-filled retirement. While we organise important family birthdays in expensive French restaurants, Ken treats himself to a plate of fish and chips and a mug of tea. It's what he likes.

I was deeply touched not by the answers Ken gave but by the ones he didn't. I suspect there was very little to say. All that needs to be said is up there in front of us, on stage. A comedy genius at work, playing his audience, unable to walk away until the last exhausted punter surrenders and heads for home.

You just know that if you toured the entire country and talked to theatre owners, entertainers, landladies and stage hands you would hear nothing but good things said about Doddy. Maybe his line of patter is not loved by everyone but the man behind it definitely is.

Of one thing we can be sure, we will never see the like of Ken Dodd again in our lifetime. He's a one-off original, never to be repeated. How many of us in his position could have resisted the temptation to act like a 'Star' and flounce around trendy London nightspots and be photographed in exotic climes with even more exotic partners, but not Doddy.

He couldn't be pretentious if his life depended on it. He doesn't play golf with Sean Connery or hob-knob with 'Parky'. He belongs to an altogether different breed of entertainer. An exclusive, all but extinct era of comedy talent that gave us the legendary Tommy Cooper and the incomparable Morecambe and Wise. Yet, even in this elevated company, there is one notable difference; Ken loves us, his audience, more than anything else in his entire world. He adores us, we are his friends, his confidants, his family and he genuinely would do anything for us and he has.

He's saved my bacon. He didn't need me or the Macclesfield Express. If he never got any more publicity in his life he'd still fill theatres … and tents … all over the country, but he remembered us here in Macclesfield and made my day.

So, 'Tatty-Bye' Ken and thanks for the call. You'll never know just 'How tickled I am'.

14 September 2000

The Phantom

Mrs B. has fallen out with me. She had been to see 'Phantom of The Opera' in Manchester with friends and was ecstatic about the whole production. Last week, she went again and finally persuaded me to go too. Unfortunately, I did not entirely share her enthusiasm and she got very cross.

I admit the singing is wonderful and the special effects are brilliant - but for those of you who have never seen it, just let me run the plot past you. See what you think.

Let's say you are Christine, a young and attractive singer and, although you are only in the chorus of an opera, you long to be the leading lady. A weird-looking guy wearing a grotesque mask, says he will tutor you to stardom. But, in order for him to do this, you must visit him in the dead of night at his home beneath the city in a labyrinth of underground tunnels. Does this sound like an offer you couldn't refuse?

Next, he falls hopelessly in love with you and proves it by murdering several members of your cast. At this point, you get cold feet and become engaged instead to a handsome young guy who still possesses all his own face.

You want to hold a celebratory engagement party but you need to ensure that the masked phantom cannot attend and ruin your night. Bearing in mind that this maniac has to wear a mask 24 hours a day – what sort of party would you organise? A wine and cheese party? A hen party perhaps? Or maybe a pyjama party? All quite safe bets. But no, you opt for a masquerade ball where everyone who attends must wear a mask!

Not surprisingly, our psychopath turns up and frightens all your friends to death, threatening Hell Fire and Damnation on anyone who does not do exactly as he says. (And he does say an awful lot!)

The police have no idea where to find him despite the fact that he keeps asking anyone who will listen to leave box five free for him every night at the opera. You run for your life and look for a safe haven. You could go and stay with your mum, or just lie out in the sun, knowing you'd be safe as houses but no – you figure the best thing to do is to visit a graveyard on your own in the middle of the night. Up pops our Phantom yet again and suggests that it is time for you to go with him beyond the 'point of no return'.

Now think about it. So far he's terrorised everyone he's ever met. He's murdered several of your friends, he's ugly as sin and he lives down a sewer. What's your answer? Would you believe this idiot of a girl actually says, "Oh alright, go on then".

Now I don't want to involve you in a domestic – but isn't this the most unlikely story you have ever heard? Be honest. That's all I ask of you.

Postscript

Well, I hope you enjoyed your journey with me through Macclesfield. What else could you have done with £6.95 anyway? Gone to McDonald's, I suppose or bought a Domino's Pizza or drunk six bottles of Bud. But at least you won't get fat reading my book — unless, of course, you ate your way through a shed load of crisps while you were doing it. But so what? Life's too short: since we're all going to die anyway — let's have a good time and die fat.

I recently attended a meeting of big film directors in Hollywood to sell the screen rights to 'Macclesfield Exposed!' and my presentation really got them going. I could actually see them starting to go after the first five minutes and by the time I'd finished they'd all gone.

I would like to thank you all for your support, I'll always wear it. Please keep sending me your letters, faxes and e-mails and I'll look forward to talking to you again in the Macc Express on Wednesdays.

Vic Barlow
Fax: 01260-253014
E-mail: vicb4sport@aol.com

Also of Interest:

PORTRAIT OF MACCLESFIELD
Doug Pickford
This illustrated book shows Macclesfield as it was, with enough information to find how "progress" has changed many buildings almost beyond recognition. An excellent souvenir of the town. £6.95

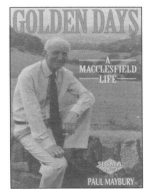

MACCLESFIELD: THOSE WERE THE DAYS!
Doug Pickford
Reminiscences from the town's residents have been collected, collated and presented by local newspaper editor Doug Pickford. Includes a wonderful collection of pictures. £7.95

GOLDEN DAYS: A MACCLESFIELD LIFE
Paul Maybury
As featured in CHESHIRE LIFE magazine. "...set to become a local best-seller" THE TOWN AND COUNTRY POST. £6.95

EAST CHESHIRE MYTHS & LEGENDS
Doug Pickford
"An author who knows his stuff; would make a delightful present; an abundance of pictures" CHESTER CHRONICLE. £5.95

CHESHIRE: SECRETS FROM THE PAST
Rodger Burgess
7000 years of Cheshire history presented in an easy-to-read style, revealing the traumatic and violent past lurking behind the peaceful façade of the county's towns and villages. £6.95

EAST CHESHIRE WALKS: FROM PEAK TO PLAIN
Graham Beech
The definitive guide to walking in East Cheshire is now in its third edition - and still outselling all other local walking guides! Completely updated and revised, the 39 walks cover 250 miles, including a 20-mile challenge route. £6.95

WEST CHESHIRE WALKS
Jen Darling
This is the companion guidebook to our East Cheshire book. The two together ensure a county-wide coverage. £6.95

CHESHIRE WALKS WITH CHILDREN
Nick Lambert
This was the first in our "walks with children" series and has quickly become a firm favourite. Things to look out for and questions to answer along the way make it an entertaining book for young and old alike. £6.95

BEST TEA SHOP WALKS IN CHESHIRE
Clive Price
Cheshire is the epitome of tea shop country - "...a winning blend of scenic strolls and tasty tea shops" CHESHIRE LIFE. £6.95

BEST PUB WALKS IN CHESHIRE
Jen Darling
This is the second edition of this well-established book which covers the entire county. Thoroughly updated, it is the most authoritative guidebook to the walks and pubs of Cheshire. Much, however, is unaltered - the same brilliant range of walks and the sparkling detailed descriptions of Cheshire's landscape and rural traditions. £7.95

A YEAR OF WALKS: CHESHIRE
Clive Price
Walk in harmony with the changing seasons. Routes from 4 to 12 miles with something special to offer for the particular time of year: Swettenham's Daffodil Dell, Audlem's canal boats in the summer, winter birds along the wilderness of the Dee Estuary or Shutlingsloe transformed by snow. £7.95

50 BEST CYCLE RIDES IN CHESHIRE
Edited by Graham Beech
"Every cyclist should be leaping into their saddles with this new book" THE CHESHIRE MAGAZINE. £7.95

TOWNS & VILLAGES OF BRITAIN: CHESHIRE
Ron Scholes
From the dawning of Neolithic man to the growth of black and white timbered market towns, Ron Scholes's knowledge of Cheshire's towns, villages, and folklore springs from his deep understanding of the county's landscape. Local historians and visitors will enjoy this informative, readable account. £8.95

Our books are available through all booksellers. In case of difficulty, or for a free catalogue, please contact: SIGMA LEISURE, 1 SOUTH OAK LANE, WILMSLOW, CHESHIRE SK9 6AR.
Phone: 01625-531035 Fax: 01625-536800. E-mail: info@sigmapress.co.uk
Web site: http//www.sigmapress.co.uk

MASTERCARD and VISA orders welcome.